The Economical Guide to Self-Publishing

How to Produce and Market Your Book on a Budget

By Linda Foster Radke
Foreword by Dan Poynter

Five Star Publications, Inc.
Chandler, Arizona

The Economical Guide to Self-Publishing:
How to Produce and Market Your Book on a Budget

Copyright © 1996, 2009, Linda Foster Radke, Chandler, Arizona

First Printing, 1996, Second Printing, May 1996, Third Printing, 2009

For information write to:

Linda F. Radke, President
Five Star Publications, Inc.
P.O. Box 6698, Chandler, AZ 85246-6698
(480) 940-8182 • Fax (480) 940-8787

e-mail: info@FiveStarPublications.com
website: www.FiveStarPublications.com

ISBN: 1-877749-16-8 (First edition)
ISBN: 1-58985-101-3; 978-1-58985-101-6 (Second edition)
Library of Congress Catalog Number: 95-092432

Library of Congress Cataloging in Publication Data:

Radke, Linda F.
The economical guide to self-publishing: how to produce and market your book on a budget / Linda Foster Radke p. cm.
Includes bibliographical references and index.
ISBN 1-877749-16-8; ISBN: 1-58985-101-3; 978-1-58985-101-6 (second edition)

Self-publishing—United States. I. Title.
Z285.5,R84 1995   95-41375
070.5.93.0973—dc20   CIP

10 9 8 7 6 5 4 3 2

First edition edited by Mary E. Hawkins
Second edition edited by Gary E. Anderson
Second edition: Book cover design by Jeff Yesh
Second edition: Book design by Janet Bergin

Acknowledgements

As a publishing consultant and small press publisher, I wear many hats, but if it hadn't been for the help of many professionals, friends, and family members, I would have had to create this book all alone. I'd like to offer special thanks to the folks who helped me with both the first and second edition.

First Edition

Thanks to:

Dan Poynter, John Kremer, and Marie Kiefer, who were willing to share their expertise.

Mary E. Hawkins, who put magic into my words. Mary has since passed on, but she stood by my side during my first years in business.

She often ended her editing assignments by saying, "Linda, the monkey is now on your back."

It's been some twenty-two years, and that monkey still follows me wherever I go!

Julie Berkel for being a grammatical wizard.

Terri Macdonald for tackling this book while pregnant with her first child.

Lisa Goldman for typing the first draft of this book and for Tai Anderson for seeing me through the second edition.

Lynlie Hermann for seeing me through the cover design.

Cass Foster, Kathleen Iudicello, and Terri Macdonald for contributing chapters.

The numerous reference librarians who answered and continue to answer my endless questions.

I'd like to thank the countless authors who trusted me to help them self-publish or partnership publish their books. I was able to help take their dream and make it come true. Their books often turned into my books and their dreams became my dreams. Together we tackled the roller coaster of taking their book to the printer and to market.

Second Edition

Thanks to:

Gary Anderson, who has done a superior job over the years of evaluating and editing many of the manuscripts that crossed my desk and who had the courage to work on the second edition of *The Economical Guide to Self-Publishing*. It takes courage to edit the words of your boss, but I hope *boss* has long since been replaced with *friend*.

Sue DeFabis, my project manager, who has stood by me since 1995. My business, and each book, is made that much better for her involvement.

Jeff Yesh, for the great job on the cover design. As he said, "This sure wasn't an economical cover!" We didn't stop until we had it just right.

Janet Bergin, for her special touch on the interior design and for having the patience of a saint.

And last, but not least, my husband, Lowell, and my sons, Gradey and Daniel, who continue to allow me to take time away from them and give it to my readers.

Table of Contents

Foreword

If you publish your own book, you'll make more money, get to press sooner, and retain control of your work. You have all the ingredients to be a successful author-publisher—**this book will be your recipe**.

Plan your product. Find a need and fill it. Target your audience before you write your book. Who are your readers and what do they want? How can you help them by delivering the most value while taking the least amount of their time? You need something to lean on—**this book will be your escort**.

Whether you self-publish or turn your manuscript over to a publisher, an author always has to do the book promotion. Most authors find out too late that publishers don't promote books.

"If it is to be, it is up to me." (William Johnston)

You need guidance and encouragement—**this book will be your coach**.

Plan your promotion before you write your book. Read this book and draft your marketing plan. You need a plan—this book will be your guide.

Writing the book is the easy part; the tip of the iceberg. The real work begins when you switch hats to expend time and money on promoting your book. As you enter new territory—**this book will be your beacon**.

Book promotion takes time. Book reviews take three months to three years to appear because magazines and even daily newspapers have long lead times. The most common mistake is to send out books for review, news releases on your book, or a direct-mail offer, and then to sit back and wait for the results. The secret of savvy book promotion is to keep up the pressure; keep sending out the packets and keep making the telephone calls. You need a constant reference—**this book will be your mentor**.

Linda Radke has made your new venture easy by providing a simple road map to economical self-publishing. Start now by taking that first step—**this book will be your secret weapon**.

Dan Poynter
The Self-Publishing Manual

Publishing is like giving birth...

Introduction

Over the years, I've been asked the same questions dozens of times. How did you get into self-publishing? How did you move from owning an employment agency to being one of thousands of publishers listed in *Literary Market Place*?

For the record, here's how all that took place. In the beginning, I owned and operated an employment service for household and childcare help. I quickly discovered that out of every one hundred calls from potential clients, only about five could afford the agency fees. That presented me with both a dilemma and an opportunity.

Of course, it was unrealistic to think I could help everyone. Although I was running a business and needed to make a profit to stay in business, I wanted to help as many people as I could—including the ninety-five percent who weren't able to budget enough money to use my company's services. So I came up with the idea of putting together a do-it-yourself kit for hiring household help.

Little did I realize that in the process of creating that first kit, I'd get hooked on publishing—to the extent of eventually selling the employment agency and moving into publishing full-time. The interesting thing was that as a publisher, I also heard more cries for help than I could fill.

My first publication, *OPTIONS: A Directory of Child and Senior Services in Phoenix, Tucson, Flagstaff, and Yuma, Arizona,* accomplished a great deal, both for people seeking household help and for me personally. It helped many families—and it brought a considerable amount of attention (and subsequently, new business) to my firm.

The agency subsidized my first publication, but I was on a very tight budget. I hired a public relations firm, headed by Toni Mattison, to help with publicity for my agency. It was one of the biggest financial risks I'd ever taken (or so it seemed at the time) and probably succeeded only because Toni was willing to work within my budget.

During our initial meeting, Toni asked many questions about my agency. She had a story set in her mind, but before leaving, I mentioned that I was putting together a kit for hiring and training household help.

"That's it," she said happily. "That's the angle we needed."

I had no idea that my first publication would lead to such a tremendous amount of local publicity—publicity that led to more potential clients and eventually to increased business. The kit created several new arenas for my agency and established me as an expert on hiring household help. It also created an increased public awareness of my agency.

Not surprisingly, several people who had purchased the kit came to my door, saying, "There's too much here that has to be done, so I'm going to let you do the job."

My experience with that kit illustrates one of the reasons for self-publishing. If you own a business and want to build that business, you have a solid basis for offering information the public needs, whether it's in the form of how-to guides, manuals, or study guide outlines for developing new skills. Once you put that information in book form, your book will often yield returns far beyond your expectations, including a pronounced increase in your credibility as an expert in your particular field.

In a nutshell, that's the story of my journey from employment agency owner to self-publisher—and to my present activity, publishing.

Of all the reasons a person might have for self-publishing, I think the two most important are *control and timing*. As the publisher, everything about your book is under your control and you have the final say in every aspect of it, including its presentation to your target audience. You can also get your information out to the public much faster as a self-publisher, which can be critical in today's rapidly changing world. You don't have to spend months querying agents and publishers or waiting, sometimes *years*, for a publisher to finally get your book into print. That can be a huge advantage.

However, you also need to understand that self-publishing your book will require a major commitment in terms of thought, energy, time, and funds. It's not an easy process, but it can have tremendous rewards if you approach it in a logical, professional manner. That's why I wrote this book—to help you maximize your efforts and minimize your mistakes.

Of course, there are other excellent guides, too, and I'd like to pay tribute to a couple of authors—Dan Poynter and John Kremer—who have written about the subject and have helped me up some steep learning curves over the years.

Expectations

What are the odds that your book will be successful? The biggest mistake novice writers make is assuming their book is going to be an instant blockbuster. Unfortunately, the odds of that happening are heavily stacked against you. If you look at bestselling author lists, you'll rarely see a first-time author or unknown person among those names. As a newcomer, it's important to be realistic in your expectations—especially if you're publishing your very first book.

Major publishers seldom succeed with just one book. They need a catalog of books to stay in business, and as a self-publisher, your catalog list will generally be very short—consisting of only your first book. As a self-publisher, you'll also be responsible for your book's promotion, marketing, and advertising, all of which will eat into your profits. So don't expect to make a lot of money on your first book—that can lead to frustration and disappointment.

It may sound harsh, but if you're going to be a successful

self-publisher, you have to enter the field with not only great information, but also with realistic expectations—and I haven't stayed in business all these years by offering my clients false hopes. Honesty is another critical factor in your ultimate success.

As I wrote this book, I found that I'm constantly discovering new ideas on how to promote and market books. This book is essentially a journal of what I've learned on a daily basis over the past twenty-plus years. I'll sometimes be referring to other leaders in various fields, because I've benefited from their advice and I want to give them due credit for the help I received from their efforts.

As a self-publisher, you're going to be wearing many hats, and in order to be successful while wearing any of those hats, you'll need to know where to find expert help. No one knows everything, and it's often much less expensive to seek out wise counsel than to make serious mistakes. In the end, their help will allow you to create the best possible book—which should always be your ultimate goal.

I wish you the very best in your efforts to become a successful self-publisher. The good news is that you've already taken the first important step—you're reading this book! Now let's explore all the aspects of how to make your self-publishing ventures all they can be.

PART ONE

I. The Manuscript

Grammar by Kathleen Iudicello
Usage
Style
Choosing a Manuscript Evaluator by Gary Anderson

II. Some Practicalities

Recorded Manuscript
Typed Copy
Role of the Editor
Choosing an Editor by Gary Anderson
"Tryout" Audience
Obtaining Permissions
Working With Independent Contractors
Art and Design
Back Cover
Parts of a Book
The Accoutrements
Copyright
ISBN Number
Bar Code

III. The Product

Print On Demand
Short Run Publishers
Typesetting by Terri McDonald
Your Publishing Options by Linda Foster Radke
Getting Printing Bids
Pricing
Final Proofs
Printing and Binding
Distributors and Wholesalers

To write...
Or not to write...

The Manuscript

Why write a book? Sound like a foolish question? Regardless of who you are, you have your reasons, whether you've analyzed them or not.

Perhaps, like me, you just want to extend your service to a larger audience. Maybe you have a remarkable person or event that you want to memorialize. You might want to record a particular piece of history. Perhaps you'd like to shed some new light on a particular subject you know well. Whatever the reason for writing your book, you've decided that you're ready to give considerable amounts of your time, talent, energy, and money to producing a book.

Once you've made that commitment, your next step is to make the fulfillment of your dream a reality—as painlessly as possible. It's going to take work and dedication, and the amount of ongoing involvement will probably be much more than you had expected, but you can do it. That's what this book is about.

The first thing you need to know is that in order for your book to be successful, it needs to fulfill not just your dream, but the dreams of many other people as well. Whether your book is a flight of fancy or a technical treatise, it must satisfy the needs and wants of many people if you're going to sell lots of copies. Regardless of your book's content, your task is to make the information enjoyable and easily understandable.

Whether you're an experienced writer or a rank beginner, the first thing to do is to get your thoughts down on paper or in your computer. You can always work on polishing your words later. The important thing is to get something down. If you're an idea person who doesn't feel capable of producing professional quality writing, you can find lots of help with that, too. There are many editors and writers who will be happy to polish your words into something you'll proud to show the world. Your first job is to organize your thoughts and then to begin writing.

Not everyone has a Ph.d. in grammar...

Grammar

by Kathleen Iudicello

Grammar – a four-letter word with seven letters. Whether writing a business letter, a proposal, or a manuscript, an author frequently experiences a feeling of insecurity.

That anxiety comes from the inevitable question most authors ask themselves: "I know the context of my work is excellent, but will my intent become muddied or my worth become questionable due to poor grammar?"

Grammar is the physical feature by which language is constructed or the set of rules that explain these constructions. Therefore, if the grammar is incorrect, the meaning of the passage may be unclear. If the meaning of a passage is unclear, the reader may have a difficult time processing the work. The last reaction an author wants from any reader is doubt due to unclear language.

What about editors? Don't most writers have editors they can rely upon to make sure that they're expressing themselves with the greatest clarity possible? Don't manuscripts have to go to an editor anyway?

The answer to both questions is yes. However, editors can be expensive. The less work they need to do, the more money a writer can keep. Therefore, a basic knowledge of grammar is necessary, whether a writer happens to be the creator of fiction or nonfiction.

Grammar has basic rules that writers from all backgrounds and all professions can easily learn and refer to for clear expression. Those rules are worth reviewing, whether by reading textbooks, attending classes, or receiving advice from other knowledgeable sources.

If you're working with an editor using hard copies (actually printed on paper), the following information will help you understand the editor's suggested corrections.

Correction symbols

abr	abbreviation; wrong abbreviation of a word
adj	adjective; wrong use of an adjective (often needs to be an adverb)
agr	agreement problem in number between a pronoun and its antecedent or a subject and predicate
awk	reads awkwardly
cap	needs capitalization
case	wrong use of a noun or pronoun to show a relationship
coord	coordination; two ideas in a sentence that aren't logically related or of equal importance; a string of clauses confusing the most important information with the supporting details
cs	comma splice; connecting two independent clauses with only a comma rather than 1) a comma and coordinate conjunction, or 2) a semicolon
dm	dangling modifier; a word or phrase meant to describe another word or phrase although that word or phrase isn't in the sentence
frag	fragment; part of a sentence that's punctuated as if it were a complete sentence
fs	fused sentence; two independent clauses joined together in one sentence with no punctuation between them (also called a run-on sentence)
ital	italicize; a word or phrase that needs to be underlined or italicized
lc	lower case; a word or phrase that shouldn't be capitalized
mm	misplaced modifier; a word (adjective or adverb), phrase, or clause meant to define another word that's not close enough to it
nsw	no such word exists

num	incorrect use of numbers; numbers under 100 and numbers that can be expressed in one or two words are generally written out, unless many numbers occur in a small portion of writing
paral	words, phrases, or clauses mixed together in a pair, list, or series to describe something (an action or a thing) but aren't all in the same grammatical form
pl	wrong use of a plural form
red	redundant
ref	confusing pronoun reference; not clear to whom or to what a pronoun is referring; a pronoun too far from its antecedent; a pronoun referring too broadly to an idea
rep	repetition isn't needed
sexist	sexist language needs to be eliminated
shift	confusing change in voice (such as from active to passive), in person (such as from third person to first person), in number (such as from singular to plural), in mood (such as from a command to advice), or in tense (such as from past to present)
sp	spelling error
split	separating a verb phrase (*I have, after today, been incorrect*) or an infinitive (*It is great to really talk*)
t	wrong verb tense
var	variety; sentences need to be varied because they're too similar in structure or length
vb	wrong verb form
ww	wrong word is used

The following are drawn correction symbols:

∧	omission
✗	obvious error
#	insert space
ℯ	delete

The following are drawn correction symbols that mean a certain punctuation mark needs to be added:

Insert hand drawn symbols

⸲	apostrophe
[ ]	brackets
⌃⌄	colon
⌄	comma
/‑‑/	dash
⊙⊙⊙	ellipsis marks
ⵏ	exclamation point
/⸗/	hyphen
( )	parentheses
⊙	period
?	question mark
⌄	quotation marks
⌃	semicolon
/	slash

There are more correction symbols that are often used to edit manuscripts, but those listed above address the most common writing errors.

— Is this font me?

Usage

"Good usage means using the right words at the right time for the right reasons," says *The New York Public Library Writer's Guide to Style and Usage*.

That book quickly adds that accomplishing this goal is easier said than done. All writers must select the level of language that will be appropriate for their readers to understand and enjoy the material. A manuscript must also follow the rules of grammar and must avoid bias. In other words, a writer must be aware of what's acceptable and what's not—even in our rapidly changing and increasingly informal culture. That means that writers must not only deal with the mechanics of writing, but also with such non-literary influences as popular culture and political correctness.

Whole books have been written on how to avoid sexist language. It's not easy to do, but there are a number of ways of recasting sentences to eliminate such language without having to resort to such ponderous phrases as: "S/he was worried about his or her standing in the community." The same philosophy applies to eliminating other types of bias, as well. It will take some careful thought, but it can be done.

There are other considerations, as well, such as the age level of your target audience. Language and material that's perfectly acceptable at one level may be completely inappropriate at another.

Regardless of your target audience and the nature of your material, you'll want it to be a grammatically perfect, nonsexist, and as unbiased as possible in order for it to achieve its highest potential.

Style

The next thing to look at is the old adage: "Take each step as far as you can go."

Organize your book as well as you can, including maintaining a consistent style and tone in your writing. What we call style in the publishing business is establishing a pattern for how you handle every section and situation over which you have a choice. For instance, what words are you going to capitalize? How are you going to handle the spelling out of numbers? (In this book, I've chosen to spell out all numbers below ten.)

To help you develop and maintain consistency, construct a style sheet at the beginning of your writing process. Most style sheets will include details on how to handle:

Abbreviations and acronyms
Capitalization
Foreign languages
Italics
Names
Numbers
Punctuation
Signs and symbols
Technical terms
Word forms (including compounding)
Special aspects

As you write, stay within the guidelines of your style sheet to maintain consistency. You can choose any authority as your guide, such as a dictionary. Among the best guides I've seen is *The New York Public Library Writer's Guide to Style and Usage*. Many editors use *The Chicago Manual of Style*, which is the dean of all style books. Another excellent guide is *Words into Type*. Helpful style sheets are also available from the Associated Press and the *New York Times*. For scholarly work, you may want to consult the *Manual of the American Psychological Association*.

Modern technology provides help with consistency. For instance, nearly every word processing program now has a "search and replace" function that allows you to change certain words or phrases throughout your manuscript with a single click of your mouse. This can be especially useful if you change your mind about a particular word, phrase, or capitalization after you're well into your manuscript.

If it seems as if I'm getting too involved with style and consistency, this will be one of your first reality checks. Readers have come to expect (and to deserve) books that conform to certain rules and conventions, and if you deviate too far from the norm, your book's sales may suffer.

Think about the signs you see as you're driving down the street. In nearly every American city the street signs look similar, if not identical, to all the others you've seen. The size, color, and shape of signs are similar because drivers are familiar with them already, which makes for a more enjoyable drive—and fewer accidents.

The same is true for books. Readers have generally read hundreds of books during their lifetimes and they expect a familiar level of consistency in order to make their reading experience as pleasant and meaningful as possible.

Testing...one, two, three...

Choosing a Manuscript Evaluator

by Gary Anderson

Gary Anderson has edited hundreds of books, ghost written dozens more, evaluated more than 1,000 manuscripts, and published four books of his own. His articles have appeared in numerous magazines and newspapers.

One of the questions I hear most often is, "How much editing will my manuscript need?"

It's a legitimate question, and one every writer needs to ask before sending a manuscript out into the publishing world, because publishing is nothing if not competitive. Your manuscript has to meet certain standards if it's going to have a chance against the competition.

One of the best ways to find out how much editing your book will need is to have someone do a manuscript evaluation. You'll find lots of people who offer them. As I always warn newbies, remember that the water is full of sharks, just waiting to swallow beginning writers whole—so do your research *before* you hire someone to do a manuscript evaluation.

Here are a few questions to ask any would-be manuscript analyst:

Will you go through the entire manuscript and make comments on the things that need to be addressed?

Will you comment on both content and mechanics, looking at the plot as well as punctuation, spelling, and grammar?

How long will it take to get the evaluation back?

How many other manuscript analyses have you done?

Can you provide references from satisfied clients?

Will you tell me exactly what my manuscript will need to make it more saleable?

When the evaluation is done, will you be able to refer me to someone who can help make the recommended changes to my manuscript?

How much will it cost?

Any person or company offering manuscript analysis should be able to answer all those questions to your satisfaction *before* you send any money. If a person's answers sound suspicious in any way, move along to the next name on your list. You may be dealing with a shark—but you generally won't know that for sure until it's too late.

Here's something else to consider: if you're getting a manuscript evaluation from a publishing company, especially a print-on-demand (POD) company, you need to understand that the person doing your analysis is being paid by that company and may not necessarily have your best interest at heart. The goal of doing your evaluation may simply be to bring in more money for the company—not to provide an honest evaluation of your book.

Here's an example from my own experience. At one point, I worked for a POD publisher as a manuscript analyst. Over a two-year period, I must admit that only about ten percent of my analyses were completely truthful. Since the company published nearly everything that was submitted, analysts were told never to discourage an author, no matter how terrible a manuscript was.

Eventually, I left that company and began doing manuscript evaluations on my own (and for companies like Five Star) that tell authors the *complete* truth about their manuscripts, followed by honest suggestions about how to make them better. Now I can truthfully say I love what I do because I'm making an honest effort to help people make their books all they can be. I tell each author exactly where their manuscript stands and then suggest one of several levels of editing.

It's vital that your book be as strong as it can be, but make sure to do your homework before you hire anyone to help make that happen, including choosing someone to do a manuscript evaluation. Remember, the water is full of sharks. Once you've found someone who is good, honest, and reasonably priced, save their number—and tell your friends—because the chances are you'll be returning for future projects.

II.

Some Practicalities

Recorded Manuscripts

Do you feel a bit timid about preparing a manuscript? You don't have to be. Consider a master mechanic who wants to create a book called *The Woman's Guide to Repairing Automobiles*. Possessing a high degree of automotive skill doesn't make that person a good writer. Even if you're not a strong writer, there are a number of ways you can effectively capture your thoughts. One of the best ways to do that is to dictate your book into a recorder.

Digital and audio recorders have gotten smaller, more efficient, and less expensive over the years, and you can purchase a good quality pocket-sized recorder today for less than $40.00. Modern recorders are also simple to use. One obvious advantage to that system is that you're not chained to your computer or to a place where you can jot down your thoughts in a notepad. As your ideas come up, all you have to do is turn on the recorder and dictate your ideas while they're still fresh in your mind.

The real expense involved with this system will come later, when someone will have to transcribe your tape and input it into a computer. That process is often followed by having an editor go through the book and bring it up to industry standards with regard to grammar, punctuation, consistency, and all the other aspects involved.

I did a great deal of the thought-gathering for this book using a minicassette recorder and I found it to be very helpful. I also owe a debt to Mary E. Hawkins, who transcribed tedious hours of tape for me as I worked on the first edition of this book.

One caveat, however, before you begin recording your book. I had an editor tell me about a fiasco she'd gone through with an author a while back. The author wanted her book transcribed exactly as she'd dictated it, but when the transcriber began working on it, she found that the author had used a recorder that was sitting on her desk and then had gotten up and walked around the room as she dictated her thoughts. In the process, sizeable chunks of the dictation were unintelligible, and therefore lost forever. That's another good reason for using a small handheld recorder.

Typed Copy

You can still use a mechanical typewriter, but a computer word processor will give you infinitely more flexibility as you begin writing and organizing your book. You can change one word or change thousands of words with a single keystroke, you can move huge blocks of text around, you can correct spelling errors, you can look for synonyms for words you use frequently—the list of advantages goes on and on. Another less obvious, but equally important, advantage is that a word processed document makes it easier for whoever will be designing your book to perform their magic—which translates to savings in terms of time, money, and frustration. There are hundreds of books on how to use word processing programs, but if you don't have the skills to do it yourself, you can always hire a competent professional to help.

Handwritten copy is usable for your notes and rough draft, but eventually you're going to want to get your words into a word processing document. Again, you can hire help if you aren't comfortable doing it yourself.

Role of the Editor

Editors have two major functions in publishing. The first is to review a manuscript and suggest reorganization or other changes. Some people in the industry call that process substantive editing. The second is to check a manuscript for grammar, punctuation, spelling, and consistency. Both types of editing will take the general tone and the purpose of your book into account. If your manuscript needs significant rewriting, you may need still another type of professional—a writer.

As a self-publisher, you'll want to cultivate an association with both types of editors (many editors can do both) and with a competent writer. They'll prove invaluable to you over the years.

Choosing an Editor

by Gary Anderson

Every day I receive inquiries from writers, many who have just finished their first book, wondering how much it will cost to edit a book before sending it off to a publisher or publishing it themselves. It's always a difficult process, and I lose a fair number of potential clients simply by being honest—but that's the way I do business. However, that's not the way many erstwhile editors you'll find on the Internet work, and regardless of whether or not I get a particular assignment, I always try to warn inexperienced authors that the water is full of sharks, eager to devour newbies. Here's my advice for keeping yourself as far as possible from the teeth of editing sharks.

First, do your homework. I can't emphasize this enough. It seems that anyone who ever took a college English class is now advertising him or herself as an editor. Before you sign a contract, check out credentials and previous experience. If they're legitimate, they'll be glad to give you references in the form of satisfied clients. If they have a website, they should also post testimonials and a list of successful projects. If a would-be editor either can't or won't offer such information, move on to the next name on your list.

If you find someone who seems legitimate and has the credentials and experience to help with your project, ask for a sample edit. Many legitimate editors will gladly edit a few pages of your manuscript at no charge, just to give you a sample of their work. I always offer to do three free pages for that very reason. An edit takes time and can be fairly costly, so you need to be certain the person you hire can do an effective job of making your words all they can be.

Make sure your potential editor has experience in your particular genre, as well. No one can edit every kind of book, no matter what they may say. For example, I simply don't know enough about the medical field to effectively edit a surgery textbook. I fully admit that, so I don't seek out that kind of work. However, I've done fiction, nonfiction, business, spiritual, science fiction, religious, and many other types of editing, and I've even done poetry, so a person can be versatile—but they also need to be honest about their limitations.

Remember that hiring someone who really knows their stuff probably will cost a bit more. After all, being good at what you do means you're worth more to your clients. I can't tell you how many times I've had to charge a client a considerable amount of money to repair a manuscript that had supposedly been edited by someone else—a shark, it turned out—who took that person's money and gave nothing usable in return.

It also means that many of the good editors will have to ask you to wait a little while before they can begin working on your manuscript. Being busy is also a sign of being good, because it means that people are seeking you out. In my own case, fully 90% of my business comes either from repeat clients or referrals—a fact I'm very proud of.

Remember, if a would-be editor is among the least expensive you've found and is ready to begin on your manuscript that very day, that should send up warning flags in your mind.

One last piece of advice about finding an editor. Although she may offer to do it for nothing, don't assume that your sister-in-law, the librarian, can edit your book just because she's around books all day and reads a lot in her spare time. Just because someone is a teacher or in some other literary field doesn't automatically mean he can edit. Being smart and educated doesn't necessarily equate to editing expertise. For instance, I've ghost-written five books for college professors who couldn't write to save their souls—but I was able to take their well thought out concepts and turn them into excellent books that found publishers almost immediately.

There are websites that can help in your search for a good editor, as well. One of the best is *Predators and Editors*, which you can find at http://anotherealm.com/prededitors/warnpa00.htm. That site lists many editing sources so you can begin your search for the perfect editor to help make your book everything you've always hoped it would be.

There are sharks in the water, there's no doubt, but that doesn't mean you have to become a victim. Do your homework and you can make your writing dreams come true.

"Tryout" Audience

Before you turn the manuscript over to an editor or anyone else, ask a few reliable people to read it. It's generally not worth asking close friends or relatives, however, because they'll often praise your work simply because they want to please you and offer you encouragement.

First ask someone who knows the field you're writing about to read your manuscript and offer feedback. Then ask the same of someone who doesn't. The knowledgeable person can offer meaningful feedback on your book's content, while the other person will be more likely to focus on consistency, mechanics, and overall flow. They can also tell you if the material is easy for a casual reader or a newcomer to the field to comprehend. As the author of the book, you're generally too close to the material to accurately judge that for yourself.

There are also a number of places that can offer professional feedback by experienced editors in the form of a manuscript analysis. Since Five Star is a partnership publisher (see my essay on partnership publishing later in this book), we insist on a manuscript evaluation for every book we consider. I believe a manuscript analysis is an excellent way to get feedback from an industry professional—although you'll need to be prepared for whatever that person may have to say, which can sometimes be less than favorable. However, if you truly want your book to be the best it can be, you have to compare it to everything else that's out there, and a manuscript analysis is a great way to do it.

Obtaining Permissions

If you decide to use information from other sources, it's critical for you to check the accuracy of everything and then to get permission to use the information. There are a number of ways to obtain permission from original sources.

One excellent way is to visit publisher websites. Even though authors usually retain the copyright to their words and publishers seldom purchase them, publishers often act as agents for their authors when it comes to granting permissions. Most publishers maintain websites these days, and you'll usually be able to click on a button that says *Permissions*. If you can't find a specific Permissions button, click on Contact Us and make your request. (For instance, HarperCollins and Simon and Shuster each have *Permissions* buttons, while you'd contact Five Star via Contact Us.)

The Association of American Publishers has compiled a list of its members' websites. You can find that list at http://www.publishers.org/member/imprints.cfm.

Literary Market Place also offers a list of publishers, either in their print version or at www.literarymarketplace.com.

Even if the book has been out of print for many years, don't assume it's automatically acceptable to use information from that book without seeking approval. Recent laws have extended copyrights for up to 120 years after the death of an author, so it's difficult to find a book that isn't protected. If you have questions about information, another good resource is the Library of Congress Copyright Office, at www.copyright.gov.

Your local public library can also be a good resource for obtaining permissions, since they have catalogs and a number of research avenues that you can explore, guided by knowledgeable librarians who are always eager to help.

I've also found the folks at www.permissionsgroup.com to be very knowledgeable and helpful in obtaining permission from the clients they represent, including some of the largest publishers in the world. They'll also tell you when you don't need to ask for permission, which is very helpful.

Working with Independent Contractors

Your manuscript may require the help of any or all of a number of professionals, including editors, proofreaders, graphic designers, illustrators, ghostwriters, typists, and computer operators. You may be able to do many of these functions yourself, but when you can't, you'll need to call for the professional help of an independent contractor.

By definition, independent contractors are persons who set their own hours, have their own equipment, work for many individuals or companies, and provide a specialized service. They generally work either out of their own offices or their homes. None of the people I regularly hire as independent contractors works in my office. They work for me and they work with me, but most of them also work with many other clients.

Using independent contractors has many advantages. It allows you to choose exactly which skills you need for a particular project and it also saves on bookkeeping, worker's compensation, and other employee-related costs.

When hiring independent contractors, do your research, ask for references and project bids, and then hire the most skilled professional you can within your budget constraints. Always spell out exactly what you need and exactly how much it's going to cost and when you can expect the job to be completed, *before* you sign an agreement with an independent contractor.

Independent contractors can often be found through their professional associations, but you'll also find lots of information online. Just type the skill you're seeking into your search engine, preceded by the word freelance, and you'll be given the websites of thousands of individuals—all looking for freelance work in their field of expertise.

Art and Design

The physical appearance and design of your book will also contribute greatly to its overall message and sales success. Artists can be expensive, but there are other less expensive possibilities, and among the most useful is clip art. (Often called *click art, stock art,* or *stock photography.*)

Clip or click art has been professionally prepared to be reproduced in various forms, and although you may have to either buy a book of clip art or pay for an individual piece of click art online, there's a great deal of both forms of art that can be used at no charge. Most art supply stores also have a collection of clip art books dealing with certain subjects, such as real estate, holidays, or sports—the list is virtually endless. As you design your book, you simply clip an appropriate illustration and position it where you want it on the page. (The same thing happens when you use click art, whether from a CD-ROM or a website.)

One word of caution, through. Just because clip art is inexpensive and easily accessible, don't get carried away and overuse it. I once had a client who had self-published his work before coming to me. It was a very good manuscript, but it was apparent that he loved clip art—because it was everywhere, to the point that it seriously detracted from the book's message. Always remember: clip art, click art, or any type of art should complement your book rather than calling attention to itself.

I used clip art for *Nannies, Maids, & More: Household Careers* and for *That Hungarian's in My Kitchen,* but I was careful to use it sparingly and always within context. It's also important to use the same type of artwork throughout your book. Consistency is critical, and mismatched artwork distracts your readers' attention from your message.

Back Cover

The back cover is both a major part of the design and an important part of a book's sales appeal. Your choices are many, but three elements most often are combined in creating effective back cover designs: a photograph and brief information about the author, an enticing description of the book's content, and laudatory quotes from well-known persons or publications.

All of those elements are designed to encourage a potential buyer scanning your book in a store to take it home. Your back cover design should be both attractive and persuasive, promising something a reader will need or want—whether it's information or entertainment.

Parts of a Book

Before you do anything about printing or typesetting, make sure your manuscript contains all the standard parts. Although you may not need all of these, here's a complete list of the parts of a manuscript, as outlined in *The Chicago Manual of Style:*

Front cover
Inside front cover
Front matter
Half-title page (this may be omitted)
Reverse blank
Title page
Copyright page
Dedication
Epigraph
Table of contents
List of illustrations
List of tables
Foreword (usually written by someone other
    than the author)
Preface and Acknowledgments (Introduction)
    by the author
Any other front matter (such as a list of abbreviations)
Main text
Back matter
Appendix
Notes
Glossary
Bibliography
Index
An About the Author page (containing a brief biography)

Inside back cover notes
Back cover
Index

A nonfiction book is more usable and marketable if it's well indexed.

"A good indexer," says *The New York Public Library Writer's Guide to Style and Usage*, "is like a good editor and serves as the reader's advocate, making the author's work accessible and comprehensible."

If you need to find an indexer, consult your editor or scan the list of indexers in the *Literary Market Place*. You can sometimes economize by contacting your local library and ask if a librarian who is familiar with indexing would like to earn some extra money. Have the person do a sample run and then establish a price. Once you've found someone who is accurate, fast, and reasonably priced, you'll probably want to use that person for future projects. As with all competent freelancers, it's good to find one you're comfortable with and become a regular client.

The index is usually the last thing to be done, because you'll have to wait for page proofs in order to specify page locations.

Copyright

You can get the latest regulations and forms from the US Copyright Office's website at www.loc.gov. Usually the copyright notice appears on the reverse of a book's title page. Other locations are permissible, but the reverse of the title page is preferred. The notice must contain the word *Copyright*, the abbreviation COPR, or the symbol ©. It must also contain the name of the copyright owner; the year of publication (when copies of the work were first placed on sale or publicly distributed).

Obtaining a copyright is a three-step process.

First, you must produce copies containing the copyright

notice, then you must publish the work, and finally, you must register the copyright notice by sending two copies and the fee to the Register of Copyrights, as specified in regulations and forms from the Copyright Office.

Another valuable service of the Copyright Office is the Library of Congress Cataloging in Publication (CIP) data, although some self-published works aren't eligible for this service. Get the latest regulations from the Library of Congress. Send requests for preassignment of Library of Congress Catalog Card Numbers to: Catalog in Publication Division, Library of Congress, Washington, DC 20540. You can also check their website for more helpful information.

There are two private companies that I've found helpful in preparing CIP, as well—The Donahue Group (www.dgi-inc.com) and Quality Books (www.quality-books.com). Visit their websites and compare pricing before making your decision.

ISBN Number

This vitally important number is assigned by the International Standard Book Numbering United States Agency. It's an individual number of a book or edition and is assigned by the R.R. Bowker Company. For forms and information about placement of the number on books, write to: ISBN U.S. Agency. R.R. Bower Company, 121 Chanlon Rd., New Providence, NJ 07974. They also have a website at www.bowker.com that contains lots of useful information.

Be wary of companies that offer to sell you a single ISBN, because that number will sometimes lead potential buyers to that company's door and not to you. This can be confusing and will often take a lot of time and energy to undo once your book has hit the street. It can also harm your overall sales.

Bar Code

These days, it's unthinkable for a product to appear without a bar code that can be read by stores and libraries. A bar code will carry your book's ISBN number, the Bookland EAN (European Article Number), and sometimes the price. Your printer may know a good source for bar codes or you can find local companies in the Yellow Pages, but there's also find lots of help available on the Internet. Just type *bar codes* into your search engine.

III.

The Product

Once you've got a satisfactory manuscript on disk, on paper, or in your word processing program, the next step is to turn it into a product—a book. You'll have to decide where to go to have your book printed, which begins with gauging how many books you'll need—and you'll want to make your dream a reality as economically as possible.

I can't tell you how many times I've had clients tell me they had thousands of books printed in order to get the per-book cost low enough to allow them to resell their books at a reasonable profit. One client told me he had purchased 5,000 hardback books—even before talking to anyone about marketing or promotion, or publicity. It was an expensive mistake—and one that you don't have to make, because you have more alternatives than ever before.

Print on Demand

Print on demand (POD) has revolutionized the publishing industry, making it easier than ever to publish your book at a reasonable cost without having to order thousands of books at a time. POD publishers archive books electronically and then use digital technology to print and bind books from those digital archives in a matter of minutes, whenever they are needed. Since there's no need to buy thousands of books in order to get a reasonable per-book price, POD should be at the top of your list when it comes to publishing your book economically. Some POD publishers even allow you to use your own imprint and set your own retail price. There are a few things you should know about POD publishers before you begin your search.

First, you'll pay more per book if you only order a few copies at a time to take to a book signing or other event. Like other types of printers, you'll get a better deal if you buy larger quantities, but you can buy one copy at a time if you want.

Second, if someone buys a copy of your book through the POD publisher's website, you'll be paid a royalty, not the entire difference between your author price and the retail price. The only time you can pocket that entire difference is on books you've bought and sold yourself. The percentage of royalties can vary considerably, so do your homework before you sign a contract.

Short Run Publishers

Another economical way to bring your book to print is to look for publishers or book manufacturers that cater to specific runs, especially those specializing in short runs (which is generally defined as a printing of less than 1,000 copies). Don't overlook quick print firms or local printers in your search. They're becoming increasingly sophisticated in meeting the needs of desktop and small-press publishers.

If you're going the short run route, it's important to first gauge the number of books you'll need. If it's a family history, you may need less than 100 copies. For more general subjects, you may need hundreds of books to fill the demand from your readers.

You'll also need to put together a list of your specifications: the number of illustrations (and whether or not they're color), any other graphics you may need, and the overall number of pages.

Printers will tell you that you'll get a better per-book price if you order larger quantities, which sounds reasonable on the surface. However, it you buy 5,000 copies of a book that sells only 500, your actual per-copy price goes way up—and you still have to decide what to do with the 4,500 copies that are cluttering up your basement or garage. It can be a costly and frustrating mistake to seriously overestimate your book's sales potential. As always, it's critical that you do your homework before you sign anything.

When it comes to the second printing of your book—if you're lucky enough to sell your entire first printing—the short run publishers actually enjoy a bit of an advantage over the POD companies. That can also be an important consideration if your book is time sensitive or covers a rapidly changing field that will require an update in a relatively short time. The reason is that the short run publisher can change just the sections of your book that need to be updated, which will save on expenses. If you need to publish an update of your book, most POD publishers will consider it a totally new project and you'll have to pay accordingly.

Another subtle, but important, advantage to selling out the first printing of a short run is that the cover of your new book can proudly proclaim, "Now in its second printing!" This will add an increased air of authenticity to your book, and your readers will be impressed that the book sold well enough to require a second printing. They don't need to know that your first run was only 500 copies. The important thing is that you successfully sold every one of them and the demand was still strong enough to warrant a second run.

One good resource for finding printers is John Kremer's *Directory of Book, Catalog, and Magazine Printers*.

Typesetting

by Terri Macdonald

Typesetting is the process by which your manuscript is prepared for the printer. Most typesetting is done on computers today, making it much less expensive and difficult than in the past. Many printing companies have in-house typesetting services. Others are listed in the Yellow Pages under *Desktop Publishing*. Make sure the typesetter you choose has experience working with large manuscripts.

There are many ways to make the typesetting go smoothly and quickly, reducing headaches for all concerned. Along with the following tips, one basic rule is to check with your typesetter on any questions or concerns you have before handing the job over.

Don't expect your typesetter to read your mind

Whether your material is handwritten, typed, or printed from a computer, it should be neat and organized.

Have everything laid out as clearly as possible. The more time a typesetter has to spend deciphering notes, putting chapters in order, and matching bits of scattered information, the more you'll be charged for the work. Ideally, you should have all materials organized in the order in which they'll appear in the book, and any graphics should be marked for insertion.

Provide a table of contents or a listing of chapter headings so the order of materials is clear.

Unless the typesetter is also your editor, expect the finished copy to be exactly as you've provided it

A typesetter won't edit for grammar, punctuation, or content unless instructed to do so. If you request these additional services, make sure the typesetter is qualified to provide them—and be prepared to pay for them. A typesetter can easily provide a spell-check, and this is always a good idea, but you or your editor will be responsible for final proofing.

Prepare your materials in order to save time and expense

If you're working on a typewriter, put in a fresh ribbon before typing your final draft. If working on a computer, check with your typesetter as soon as possible before you put your manuscript on disk or send it by email. The best assurance of compatibility between two systems is to put a sample on disk (or send it in an MS-Word file, if your typesetter accepts emailed files) and have your typesetter take a look at it. Chances are, the typesetter won't charge you just to check compatibility. The typesetter will pull the file up on screen and tell you if it comes in clearly. (Most typesetters are accustomed to working with MS-Word documents, so if you're working in Word, you can be fairly certain that your files will be compatible, although it never hurts to ask.)

Unless your system and program are identical to your typesetter's, your best bet is to save the file as an ASCII file. This option should be available in the save function of your word processing program and will prevent unnecessary information from being included in the file. Here's a sample of what a file can look like if improperly saved:

¡ ¡ -¡ ¡ à h # ¡ ¡ ? ? . (¡ ¡ - @ a * ¡ ^ (Ø Æ * ¨ ? # fj q Ú 3 ¡ (a6Par √ ¡ ? $ @ ¡ ¡ ? ? - ¡ # ø ? ?

The time involved in clearing up a file like this could greatly increase the cost.

Your manuscript can be scanned electronically

If your manuscript exists in printed form, but not on disk—perhaps it was produced on a typewriter or a computer file that has been lost or corrupted—it can be scanned as text through a scanner. The resulting text file can then be manipulated and formatted as any other text file would be. The important thing is to provide a clean copy with crisp, dark type to the scanner operator. It's a good idea to try a sample page to see how well it scans before committing to an entire project. Always be sure to spell-check and proof the finished product for scanning errors.

Don't waste time formatting your text

By *formatting*, I mean indenting paragraphs, bolding or italicizing, or centering headlines. Simply insert a return after each paragraph or heading. Don't add extra spaces or tabs. The typesetter will be developing style sheets that will spell out the characteristics of each paragraph, heading, subheading, or footnote.

By using programmed style sheets, a typesetter can change characteristics of an entire document with a few simple commands. Accordingly, any formatting you've done will have to be removed in order to prevent it from interfering with the style sheet commands. These commands also provide uniformity and consistency throughout the book. If there are certain phrases or passages you want formatted in a specific way, let your typesetter know or provide a marked-up copy of the manuscript with formatting directions noted.

Get samples

Unless you're familiar with the industry, you most likely won't know what options are available in the way of type and formatting. Ask your typesetter for several samples. This can be done easily and quickly. Make sure your choice is readable and clean-looking. Your type choice may depend on final output.

Graphics and special effects

Most typesetters will have clip art and decorative elements available. A little ornamentation can go a long way toward making your book more attractive. Consider adding a simple ornament to your chapter headings, end of chapters, or page numbers.

If you have specific images in mind, it may take some research to find suitable art. You can find lots of clip art at graphic art supply stores and online, but you can't find anything suitable, you can pay your typesetter to find it for you. Another option is to hire an artist to create exactly what you want. Ask your printer or typesetter for references. There's wonderful talent available at reasonable cost. Be as specific as possible to save time and money.

Final output

When you're completely satisfied with your manuscript, your typesetter will produce a final copy from which the printer will make plates for printing your book. This final output can take several forms. It may be printed on standard white paper from a laser printer, on resin-coated paper at a higher resolution from an imagesetter, or on film (similar to the type used in cameras and processed in the same way to become negatives, from which printing plates can be made).

Some printers will produce the final output in-house. In this case, the typesetter will provide the manuscript to them, either on a disk on online. The printer will then output the file to film, from which the printing plates will be made.

The cost of these choices can vary greatly. Laser output, the least expensive option, is suitable for some books. If your book is mostly text, with simple solid black and white graphics, you may be able to use laser output. If your book contains photos or screened images (graphics with shades of gray), you'll need to have your file output to film for the best results. Your printer can advise you as to the best method for your book.

Your Publishing Options

An article by Linda Foster Radke

Writers who find themselves caught in the publishing dilemma of "should I wait eons for a standard publisher to pick up my manuscript or go out on a limb and self-publish?" will be glad to learn that there's a middle-of-the-road publishing option: partnership publishing. To understand partnership publishing, however, it's important to review the other commonly used publishing methods.

Standard Publishing

With *standard publishing*, a publishing company selects the manuscripts it will publish. The publisher absorbs all the costs and risks of printing and distribution, so it maintains strict editorial and creative control over every phase of a book's production. The author is paid a nominal royalty, usually a percentage of a book's net proceeds.

After being accepted, it commonly takes 18–24 months from the date the contracts are signed before a book will actually be seen in print—but that's just the beginning. While standard publishing companies maintain marketing departments, most first-time authors don't realize that the average publisher's budgets is restricted, so each author is expected to assume part (and sometimes a large part) of the responsibility for marketing a book.

Self-Publishing

With *self-publishing*, the author maintains complete editorial and creative control over a book's production, but also absorbs all the associated costs and risk. The author is fully responsible for everything, including design, printing, marketing, distribution, and sales. Although a self-published book can appear on bookshelves in as little as three months, it's not likely to show up on bookstore shelves that soon.

First-time self-published authors often run into roadblocks when it comes to securing distribution by the big houses, such as Baker & Taylor or Ingram, from whom bookstores like Barnes & Noble and Borders purchase. A number of costly mistakes can be made along the way, too, such as a poor cover design, inferior printing quality, the omission of a barcode, not realizing the time commitment necessary for effective public relations, not knowing where or how to market a book, or simply paying too much for printing or marketing materials.

Partnership Publishing

The middle-of-the-road alternative is *partnership publishing,* in which the author and the publisher agree to split the cost and risk of publication and distribution, as well as proportionally share any revenues generated by sales. The author and the publisher have equal voices as they make their way through the often confusing maze of editorial and creative decisions. They also share in the marketing of the book, because each of them has a stake in the book's success.

As an added advantage, partnership-published books usually will get into the hands of more readers—in a shorter amount of time—than standard or self-published manuscripts. Since partnership publishers seldom have manuscripts stacked to the ceiling waiting to be reviewed, they can get to yours faster; and since partnership publishers won't be assuming the entire financial risk, they can afford to take chances on edgier material and unknown authors. On the other hand, because they'll be sharing the financial burden, partnership publishers still must choose books that are marketable, which means rejection is a possibility.

Although a self-published book can be delivered shortly after paying the printer's bill, a partnership-published book usually connects with readers quicker because the author can draw on a publisher's experience in marketing, distributing, and sales strategies. When combined with the author's own efforts, there are two promotion avenues being pursued at the same time, which can be a big advantage in terms of sales.

"When I was the community relations coordinator for Borders Books and Music, I saw firsthand that it was nearly impossible for a self-published author to get a book accepted into the store. There were just too many obstacles," says Lynda Exley, who partnered with Five Star Publications to publish her eleven-year-old son's book, *The Student from Zombie Island: Conquering the Rumor Monster.* "I also saw many poorly designed error-ridden self-published books that authors had poured their life savings into. These were basic mistakes that any good editor or publisher could have prevented."

However, as a member of several writers clubs, Exley says she was also privy to many horror stories about books taking several years to be accepted by a traditional publisher, followed by a couple more years before actually being printed, only to receive a minimal amount of marketing attention from the publisher.

Exley adds, "Unless you're Stephen King, a traditional publisher isn't going to cover expenses, like traveling to book signings or additional marketing beyond the initial few press releases. That money comes out of any miniscule royalties paid to the author."

After meeting with Five Star Publications and learning about partnership publishing, Exley realized that it represented the best of both worlds.

"We share the expenses, the workload—and the profits," she says. "Five Star gives me all the benefits of a big publisher—editing services, distribution with Baker & Taylor and Ingram, promotional materials, a dedicated website, and publicity—along with all the advantages of self-publishing, like a higher profit margin, creative control, and a shorter time period from inception to print."

For Exley, it's been a win-win situation from the beginning, and has several benefits she hadn't expected.

"Linda Radke became a mentor to me. Through her direction, I've learned more about publishing, marketing, and selling than I'd ever dreamed, and she's right there in the trenches with me, selling The Student From *Zombie Island*."

There are many other advantages, too, says Exley.

"I also get a discount on promotional materials. Linda's been in the industry nearly thirty years and has established suppliers that give her the best prices, which she passes on to me. I save money on trade shows, too, since other authors share space under the Five Star roof, which reduces the cost for all of us. Five Star also developed and maintains a website, www.ZombieIslandBooks.com, that's way beyond what we could have done on our own. A traditional publisher wouldn't have done that for a low profile client like me."

Exley also points out that partnership publishing earns her book more respect from bookstores and the media.

"I can proudly say that *Zombie Island* was accepted and published by a legitimate, bona fide publisher instead of shouting 'self-published' to everyone who sees it. Those are words that no bookstore or media personality wants to hear. It's not that self-publishing is a bad thing or that it automatically means a book is inferior. There are some wonderful self-published books out there. However, because inferior self-published books are plentiful, self-published books simply don't get the same respect that traditional or partnership-published books receive. Partnership publishing has opened doors for me that wouldn't have been possible otherwise."

To learn more about partnership publishing or Five Star Publications, visit www.fivestarpublications.com or call 480-940-8182.

Getting Printing Bids

If you choose the POD route, getting prices is a simple matter of visiting a number of websites to compare packages. Getting bids from standard printers can be a bit more difficult, but can be well worth the effort.

First, be realistic about your product. If you're writing a manual that will need to be revised regularly, don't visualize a coffee table book. If your book is designed to receive heavy use over several years, such as a reference book, it will need to be able to withstand that hard usage. Also, your cover will need to be professional-looking and appealing to potential readers.

Besides price, you'll also want to know how long it will take a printer to get your finished order back to you. A printer that does nothing but books may often be able to offer a shorter time frame than a more general printer. In fact, many book manufacturers listed in *Literary Market Place* include turnaround time in their entries. It's important to weigh price/copy vs. delivery time carefully, since it's often not worth saving 25 cents a copy if you have to wait an extra six to eight weeks—especially if your material is timely.

In response to your request for a bid, printers indicate how they'll meet each requirement, prices for various numbers of pages (if you're not sure, which will often be the case) and for various quantities. If you plan to use a POD publisher, you'll want to find out about per-copy prices, how many books you need to order at one time to receive a price break, and how long it takes to receive your copies. Printers will also specify time, shipping costs, packing methods, and any other information about getting the books to you.

Don't hesitate to get more than one bid. Not only will prices vary, but printers may make valuable suggestions that you have not considered. Pay particular attention to quantity prices. Don't be overly optimistic in estimating how many copies you're going to sell. If you sell out your first printing, we've already talked about the advantages of being able to do a second one. Smaller quantities also make sense for time sensitive material.

Pricing

If your publisher gives you a choice (many POD companies don't), think carefully before you set a price for your book. It's difficult to make a profit from your first book. Once it's back from the printer, you'll often have to give distributors and retail outlets discounts of 40–60 percent off the book's retail price. You'll also have to provide free review copies to the press and the media, and you'll have to create media kits, including fliers and press releases, to help generate publicity for your book. According to self-publishing guru Dan Poynter, all of that can run eight times the production cost for books sold through the mail and retail stores and five times the production cost for textbooks.

The bottom line: be realistic. You probably won't get rich from your first self-published book. The best philosophy is to publish your book as economically as you can while still creating a quality product. Then use that book for promotion, publicity, and marketing in every way possible—for your own personal recognition as well as for income.

Final Proofs

Final proofs are often called bluelines. These are meant to show you exactly how the pages of your book are going to look after they're printed. Since these proofs are made from the camera-ready copy, it's expensive to make changes at this point, which emphasizes the importance of having your book carefully edited and proofed before you begin the publishing process. The proofs will also show the positioning of illustrations and graphics. This isn't the time for heavy editing, but it does give you one last chance to catch any errors or misplaced graphics. Never allow a book to be printed without bluelines. They're not something to be skipped.

Before you receive your bluelines, your printer will send you *galley proofs*. The name comes from the old days of setting type in a long tray (called a *galley*) and then pulling a copy for proofreading. Today, galleys are proofs that can be sent to reviewers who need to see copies in order to meet their own deadlines. Galleys are often less finished than blue-lines, with pages less completely set up, but the copy itself will be complete.

Printing and Binding

Don't be tempted to economize on printing and binding.

Ask yourself, "How will this book be used, shelved, stored?"

One mistake I made in my very first publication was to have it spiral bound. It couldn't be marketed to librarians because it had no spine showing the title. It was also difficult to shelve. Later, I published a cookbook that had two types of binding. One part of the order had a plastic coil binding, which was great for cookbooks that need to lie flat. The other part of my order had perfect binding to be sold to people and institutions that were more concerned with being able to shelve the book easily. If you're using a quick print firm or short run publisher, you'll have many choices of bindings, but always take the book's use and the purchaser's needs into consideration before making your decision.

The most common form of binding these days (especially among POD publishers) is perfect binding with a paperback cover. In perfect binding, the pages are tightly glued onto a squared-off cover, which provides a spine for the book title. (The book you're reading right now is perfect bound.)

For hardback books, there are several types of bindings and choices regarding both price and durability. Look at a dictionary or other book that gets hard usage and you'll see not only a hardback, but groups of pages (called signatures) that are gathered and sewn, then pulled together, often with a head cloth inside the cover. Producing hardbacks costs more than paperbacks, they require more room, and they weigh more, which means higher shipping costs.

Distributors and Wholesalers

If you expect to need national distribution of your book, look into the services of wholesalers and distributors. Even if you decide to perform one or both of those functions yourself, you'll need to know what each of them can and can't do for you.

Distributors usually accept books on consignment. That is, they handle book orders or fulfillment for you and pay only after the book is sold. Some distributors issue catalogs and have sales representatives who call on prospective buyers in libraries and bookstores. Unfortunately, it's difficult to judge in advance how vigorous a distributor's sales efforts will be. Well-known distributors, such as Quality Books and Unique Books, target librarians in their sales efforts. Their representatives visit libraries and open accounts for selling books.

Wholesalers stock your book and fill orders for their clientele. Baker & Taylor and Ingram are two well-established wholesalers.

If you're working economically and following an order-on-demand policy, you can easily serve as your own distributor. Remember, however, that may mean physically fulfilling all orders and taking care of all bookkeeping if your POD plan does not.

Both wholesalers and distributors will expect you to do publicity, promotion, and marketing on your book and to keep them informed of your efforts. Carefully study the contracts offered by either wholesalers or distributors, and always ask for references of previous satisfied clients.

The *Literary Market Place* lists distributors and wholesalers, as well as giving an overview of their specific spheres of influence. Other reference works, such as John Kremer's *1001 Ways to Market Your Book* and Dan Poynter's *The Self-Publishing Manual*, also describe the services of several wholesalers and distributors.

You'll also find the addresses of some major firms in the Appendix.

PART TWO

I. The Business of Books

Running a Business from Your Home
The Lion's Share of Profits: The Benefits of
    Self-Publishing by Spencer Gorin
Banking
Establishing a Business Name
Your Logo
Zoning
Telephone Service
Telephone Equipment
Toll-Free Number
Phone Book Listing

II. Equipment

Computer
Order Forms
Invoices
Prospect List
Fax Machine
Photocopier

III. Procedures

Payment and Prepayment
Shipping
Freight Collect
Filing System

IV. Expanding Your Business

The Business of Books

"Writing is an art, publishing is a business," says Mark Ortman in *A Simple Guide to Self-Publishing*. Self-publishing is a business—but it's often a business that a person just falls into without any real preparation or planning, which is a formula for frustration and potential disaster. Things can quickly get out of hand if you don't conduct every phase of your publishing business as a commercial endeavor.

Running a Business from Home

For at least your first book, you'll probably be running your business from home. There are many books that offer excellent details on working from home, and I'd recommend that you read as many of them as you can, because setting up a home office requires planning, determination, and discipline.

When I first started my household employment agency, I ran the business from my home, but I soon began getting phone calls at all hours of the day and night, which was great for business, but it did nothing to preserve the sanity of my family. Therefore, within a month I opened a separate office in order to keep the peace.

Some businesses lend themselves more readily than others to being run from home, and publishing is definitely one of them. You can easily run your self-publishing business from your home without giving up your day job. In fact, I recommend that you do just that until you're making enough money to begin devoting full-time hours to your publishing efforts.

There are several things to remember as you begin your self-publishing business. First, maintain a professional image in everything you do, whether it's maintaining business hours, answering the phone, sending out flyers, or developing a website.

Maintaining regular business hours is important so you don't feel like a slave to your business—and to remind you not to work night and day, since every day should also include family time. In addition, keeping regular hours discourages people from calling you at all hours simply because they know you work at home.

Of course, the line between business and family will sometimes get blurred when you work at home, but it's important to separate the two as much as possible. It's also critical to take time away from your business on occasion so you won't burn out. Taking a little time off allows you to return to your business refreshed and ready to go again. You may also need to hire part-time help, rather than letting your business encroach upon too much of your time.

It's even more difficult to run a home business if you have small children, but there are a number of organizations that can offer suggestions and networking opportunities. Check your phone book or go online if you need help.

In my experience, establishing regular business hours allows me to process incoming orders, queries, and correspondence while also developing new approaches for publicity and marketing. In fact, the fewer incoming demands I have, the more time I can spend prospecting and reaching to a larger audience.

With the advent of home computers, fax machines, cell phones, laptops, and other electronic aids, conducting a business from home is easier and more appealing than ever before. Check your local library, the Small Business

Administration, or your computer search engine for a wealth of reference material. The more you know about how to run your business economically and efficiently, the better your chances of success.

The Lion's Share of Profits: The Benefits of Self-Publishing

By Spencer Gorin, co-author, with Charlie Steffens, of Learning to Play, Playing to Learn

The first edition of our book, *Learning to Play, Playing to Learn*, was published by one of the major publishing companies. We sold a fair number of copies and received a small royalty. The publishing company made a fair amount of money from our book and we, in turn, got an advance and got international sales that we might not have gotten otherwise. However, it soon became apparent that the promises of marketing and media opportunities that the publisher was going to arrange were never going to materialize. The majority of marketing efforts were really left up to us, the authors.

After a few years, that publishing company was sold to an even bigger one. At first, we were excited about the possibilities. The new company had a greater reach into educational markets, which were our target audience, but once again we learned a frustrating lesson. Our book seemed to have gotten lost in the shuffle of moving from one company to the other. Additionally, a few years after the initial printing, we were no longer considered a focus of interest by the company, even though sales (which were mostly generated directly by us and our clients) continued to be financially sound.

Luckily, we were able to secure the rights to our materials and to then self-publish our book, which came in handy when we did a major revision ten years after its initial publication. We no longer had to satisfy a major company that wanted to water down our book in order to appeal to a larger audience—yet didn't actively promote or market it.

The majority of our sales still come from educational and youth-servicing professionals who attend our trainings and workshops or visit our website, www.joyinlearning.com. The good news is that instead of making a very small royalty percentage, we now receive the lion's share of the profits, which only seems fair, since we're still doing the lion's share of the marketing. (As you might imagine, fair play is important to us!)

Banking

One of your first business contacts will be your bank. You'll need a separate bank account called a merchant account. This is especially true if you're planning to accept electronic payments or if you will be making electronic deposits.

The biggest challenge for the person running a business from home, including self-publishers, is a bank's reluctance to issue a merchant account to a home address. Banks are afraid of getting returns from a home business. For instance, if a publisher refuses to refund money to a buyer, the bank is left to handle the dispute. If your bank officers balk, one way to win them over is to ask for a trial period. That will allow you to show your commitment to conducting your business in a professional manner.

Having an excellent credit history and good references from other lenders will help, too. Your bank's transaction rate will generally be based upon your volume of business, so you can expect to pay a higher rate until you're able to generate enough business to qualify for a reduction. Rates can vary widely, so as with every other aspect of your business it will be worth your while to shop around.

If you're accepting payments via credit cards, you'll also need the equipment to transfer these payments directly to the bank. This often means buying or renting special equipment, including a printer that prints receipts and a machine into which you enter credit card information. Some banks will set up a merchant account but will charge up to $700 for the necessary equipment. Renting the equipment can be cheaper, but you'll be paying those fees every month you're in business. You can sometimes find used equipment, and though bankers won't generally volunteer the information, they might tell you if they know where you can find used equipment if you ask.

Another advantage of accepting credit cards electronically is that you can transfer the funds into your account immediately, rather than having to go to your bank to make deposits.

It looks impressive to include an electronic receipt when you're sending out a book order that someone has charged. It adds to the professionalism of the transaction.

Many businesses are now beginning to use PayPal, as well. If you do much shopping on eBay, you're probably already familiar with PayPal (in fact, PayPal is owned by eBay). PayPal accounts are easy to set up, require no special equipment, and the fees you'll be charged to accept credit cards are generally comparable to those you'd pay your bank. Check www.paypal.com for more information.

The folks at Costco offer are very competitive in the helping you establish a merchant account. You need to sign up for a business account, but it will be well worth your time to do this research.

We recently started processing our charges through our QuickBooks accounting program. It simplifies the process and is well worth the extra charges we pay.

Establishing a Business Name

Never forget: self-publishing is a business, and a business needs to an identity if customers are going to find it, so choose your business name carefully. Your business needs a name that will lend prestige, but avoid any connotation that might result in less than complete respect for you and your product. Self-publishing has always carried a certain stigma in many people's minds, although that perception is changing as the industry evolves. That's a big reason why choosing a business name will require some genuine consideration.

First, the name should be unique, which means doing some research. If you've got an idea for a potential name, you can start with *Literary Market Place* to see if the name has already been used. Then, if you don't see it there, you can type the potential name into your search engine to see what types of entries appear.

Why should your name be unique? Many years ago, when I was naming my agency, I was advised that selecting a name similar to another business can potentially create problems. For instance, if a publisher with a similar name gets sued, you could get pulled into a lawsuit. Having a similar name could also confuse buyers, limiting the effectiveness of your advertising and lowering your sales. That similarly-named business might publish something controversial that generates negative publicity and reflects badly on your business.

Given the potential problems, it's important to check out a proposed name thoroughly before you decide to use it— but you also want to think ahead during your deliberation process. You may not want to mark your turf too specifically. If you plan to publish only within a certain genre and to establish your company as the authoritative publisher in a particular field, you'll want to choose a name that reflects that intention. On the other hand, if you're planning to self-publish a number of books of your own, you might want to use your name in your business name (such as *Linda Foster Radke Publications*). Many self-published authors have used this strategy very effectively over the years. However, if you're an unknown author (and the chances are good that you are, since you're reading this book), there's a good reason for not using your own name as part of your company's name. If you're fortunate enough to be successful in your efforts, you may find a larger publisher that's interested in buying your business. Using the example from the previous paragraph, Linda Foster Radke Publications would lose a considerable part of its appeal to a potential buyer if I wasn't going to remain involved in the firm. Selling a company with a more general name wouldn't create that problem.

If you're planning to diversify, and especially if you're planning to eventually publish books by other authors, you'll want to choose a more generic name. I knew a man whose first book had a delightful ethnicity, so he set up his self-publishing business under a name that reflected that fact. Initially, the company's name added to the charisma of his first book. However, the content of his second book was light years away from his first one, and the company name he'd created did little to generate sales—in fact, it probably had the opposite effect.

Once you've done your research and have chosen a name, find out what you have to do to register that name in your particular state. For instance, in Arizona, I had to contact the secretary of state.

Your Logo

Not only must your name be unique and easily remembered, but it also must be easily translated into graphic presentation. That is, it must look good on your letterhead, order forms, and all other business-related materials. If you create a logo (an identifying symbol, piece of art, or letter arrangement), be sure it will enlarge and reduce well and reflects the personality of your business. For my own publishing firm, I chose the name *Five Star Publications* and added a lighthearted figure as part of our logo—one that lends itself well to various reproduction sizes or colors.

I've used one economical way to create a logo very successfully over the years. For my employment agency, I employed an art student who had recently graduated, and she did a wonderful job. If you contact a local art school, university, or even a high school, you'll often find some extremely talented people. If time isn't of the essence, an art teacher can sometimes use the creation of your logo design as a class project. Not only will you get a logo, but students will also gain experience in logo creation. The winning student will be able to add a professional piece of work to a portfolio.

Whether you work with an artist or a class, come to terms up front about charges and payment so there are no surprises later. Give the artist some type of direction and show a few logos that look interesting to you. You don't want exact copies, but showing logos you like will give the artist an idea of what you're looking for.

When designing a logo, your first consideration should

be the effect it will have on the people who see it. It doesn't need to contain all pertinent information, but it should be unique enough to be recognizable at a glance. A great logo will go a long way toward creating your company's image and prestige, so give it careful thought.

You also might want to consider a slogan to go along with your logo. We use "Your Story Begins Here," and when you see our logo, you'll also see our slogan. It's double branding.

Zoning

Along with establishing a name for your business and deciding whether or not to conduct it from home, you'll need to check the zoning regulations in your area. Are there specific restrictions against home businesses? Generally a self-publisher or small press will have no problems with zoning, but it's wise to check before you begin.

Telephone service

Will your personal telephone service be adequate for your self-publishing business? Perhaps, but perhaps not, especially if you eventually see yourself publishing several books.

Having the name of your publishing company and your city and state listed will make it easier for someone to call for information and get your telephone number, which means you'll probably want to consider a specific business phone number versus using your residential line. If you have a residential phone number and don't divulge that it's also used as a business line, you may lose the opportunity to have your company listed in the business section of either the White Pages or the Yellow Pages of the phone book. Check with your local phone provider to see what their regulations are.

Another consideration is how the phone will be answered, especially if you have children. Nothing blows a professional image more quickly than to have your six-year-old answer a business-related call. If you want to maintain a professional image, you want to have every business call answered in a businesslike fashion.

Your main phone number should be a business line, but your fax line could be done through your residential service. This saves money on phone bills.

Telephone Equipment

Here's an economical way to get started with your business phones: combine your business line with your toll-free number, which eliminates the need for a second line. You can do that by having your local phone company set up your phone lines with custom rings. Depending on the sound of the ring, you'll instantly know which number the caller is using.

Having a phone with a hold button and speed dial can also be worthwhile. Modern technology allows you to program dozens of numbers, all available at the touch of a button.

Toll-Free Number

It's no longer expensive to maintain a toll-free number—and a toll-free number can be a great sales tool. Many people won't call a long distance number just to get information, but they'll gladly call a toll-free number for that same information. If your business depends upon talking to people on the phone, you want as many calls as possible—and a toll-free number can help you accomplish that goal.

By looking in the Yellow Pages or going online, you'll find many companies that can set you up with a toll-free number. As with every other aspect of your business, interview several companies before you make a decision—and don't consider price alone. Reliability is also critical to your success. Losing just one client could be enough to pay a month of toll-free service.

Phone Book Listing

Should you be listed in the Yellow Pages? It will be easier for someone to contact you, but in today's world it may not be as necessary as it was in the past. This is especially true for a self-publisher, since most of your business will be done either over the phone, via fax, mail order, or on the Internet. Therefore, consider the cost of a Yellow Page listing versus the amount of business it will generate. In many cases, you'll find that it may not be nearly as important to your publishing success as it might have been several decades ago.

In my own case, advertising my household employment agency in the Yellow Pages was a major part of my budget. However, as a publisher, I now find that a simple line listing is sufficient for my local needs. I spend a great deal more on maintaining an Internet presence, which reaches a worldwide audience and brings in the vast majority of my work.

In time...
you will learn to
love your computer.

Equipment

In order to give you a feel for the kinds of operating equipment you may need, even if you only plan to publish one or two books, let's look at the equipment I use.

Computer

First of all, every business needs a computer, even if it's only to keep records and accounting files. We've already discussed the computer's role in word processing, so let's consider the computer's other uses in your business operations.

To select the computer that's best for you, visit a store that specializes in computers and software and tell them exactly what you're hoping to accomplish. Since they're computer specialists, they'll be able to set you up with hardware and software that you might not have been aware of.

I don't encourage you to buy used computer equipment. Computers go out of date too quickly in today's world and the cost of new computers continues to go down, accompanied by a rapid increase in the quality of both hardware and software. So even if someone offers you what sounds like a great deal, I recommend buying a new computer that's been loaded with all the components and programs you'll need to accomplish your goals.

If budget is your main concern, you might consider a refurbished computer. Companies like Dell sell refurbished units or units that were returned and are therefore unable to be sold as new. Returned computers often have extra goodies that you won't need to pay extra for. I'd recommend talking to a sales person instead of just buying online because they'll sometimes give you an even better deal to earn your business. Make sure your unit is insured, and pay the extra cost for an extended warranty.

Printers

If you have a computer, you'll also need a printer, and I've discovered a great way to save money when selecting a printer. I used to look for the best buy on a printer, but it took years for me to realize that what I should have been doing was pricing printer cartridges first and then looking at the printer itself.

There are many kinds, but I've found that a laser printer gives me more for my money and actually costs less per page in the long run than an inkjet printer. I also like all-in-one printers because they take up less space and can easily take care of most of my quick printing needs, including scanning and faxing.

Another thing I recommend is an onsite maintenance policy, especially if you buy a laser printer. You generally can't afford to be without a printer while your machine is out of commission.

There are also some credit card companies that will add an additional year of coverage if you purchase a printer using their card. That extra coverage extends beyond your printer's original warranty. It's an option worth considering. Check with your credit card provider to see if they offer extended warranties. It could save time, frustration, and expense.

Computer Consultant Sources

Even if you're a complete novice, you need a computer for your business. Don't be intimidated if you're not a computer expert. Over the years, computers have gotten much easier to use, and if you're unsure of your ability, there are many classes available at community colleges, online, at computer schools, and through night school programs.

If you still don't feel comfortable, you can hire a computer consultant. It will be more expensive than doing it yourself, but at least you'll know that a consultant will be familiar with a variety of software programs that can help you achieve success. Stop struggling and get help. You can even hire a consultant to personally walk you through a particular program you'll be using often. Two hours of one-on-one time can raise your confidence level considerably, which makes good use of your time and money.

When I first hired a consultant to come to my office and teach me some of the basics of a word processing/business program, I prepared a list of specific topics I needed help with and it worked out quite nicely. After several hours of one-on-one consulting, I only needed a few follow-ups on the phone to get going. The time involved (and the expense) wasn't much and I was pleased with the results.

To economize, you could visit your local college and put a note on the bulletin board of the computer lab saying that you'd like to hire someone to teach you a particular program. College students are generally eager to earn a little extra money and they're often fluent in the most popular software programs. This can be an excellent way to hire expert advice without paying top dollar (often college students will work for less than half what it would cost for a professional consultant)—and it will save hours of frustration and aggravation.

Another possibility is to hire a college instructor who does freelance work on the side. It may cost a little more than hiring a student, but the savings will still be significant compared to a full-time computer consultant. You can economize even more by telling the instructor that you're willing to visit the computer lab for your classes. That way, you won't have to pay for travel time or other related expenses, since the hourly rate is usually less if an instructor doesn't have to come to your place of business.

If you still aren't sold on the need for a computer of your own, you can schedule time on computers in libraries for free or rent computer time at print shops. Check into per-hour cost and the type of programs loaded into the computer.

If nothing else, working on someone else's computer will allow you to gain experience and raise your confidence level. You may even discover that having to make appointments and being limited as to how much time you can work will help you make the decision to get a computer of your own.

In larger cities, there are also commercial businesses that rent computer time. Go online or check your local Yellow Pages for location and cost.

Here are a few of the business uses for which I find my computer particularly helpful and timesaving:

Order Forms

I have my computer set up to do all the calculations for my orders. It figures in any discounts, my dealer cost, list price, and even the sales tax I have to charge for all Arizona purchases. (If someone from outside of Arizona makes a purchase, the program doesn't add the sales tax.)

Invoices

My computer completes these forms. As you begin to publish more books, including a second or third book, you're going to need to keep good records

For example, I can go through the computer and do a search for anyone who purchased a copy of *Nannies, Maids & More*. If I have another book coming out that's geared toward the same audience, I can go through my computer database, get a listing of all the customers who purchased the previous book, and send them a promotional package for the new title.

Prospect List

You can also enter potential customers in your computer database. For example, if someone requests information about a cooperative mailing, I can put the name in my computer base as a prospect for my next cooperative mailing. Even if that person didn't participate in the first mailing, I still have the name and address in my database for future mailings.

Fax Machine

In order of importance, after the telephone and computer comes my fax machine. For me, getting a fax machine was a major decision and a major investment—even though they've greatly come down in price since then. Once I bought one, I hooked my new machine to our main business telephone line—but quickly discovered that it wasn't a good idea. There was just too much conflict between the two uses of our phone line.

Now I highly recommend that you get a separate fax line. To save money on your second line, maintain a business listing for your main line (to ensure your Yellow Pages listing) and use a residential line for your fax machine. Residential rates are cheaper and you don't necessarily need a Yellow Pages listing for your fax line.

If your fax machine happens to be in your home (and it probably will be, at least at first), you can get a private line for your fax number along with your residential line. Believe me, using a designated fax line will simplify your business life a great deal.

A fax machine also comes in handy when you're sending out press releases. You'll also receive requests via fax for review copies of your books. Just recently, I received a request from Rome, Italy. A magazine called Colors wanted to review a client's book, so they faxed me their request. Many reviewers will also request additional information via faxes, so having a fax machine can make your life easier and more profitable.

Remember—all-in-one printers also include a fax component.

Photocopier

Another indispensable piece of equipment is a photo-copier. I bought a new copier when I outgrew my small one. For my second machine, I bought a used copier, but I purchased a maintenance agreement at the same time—something I've never regretted. In publishing, you'll find that you need a copier almost as much as you need your files and your computer, to the point where you'll go into panic mode if your copier breaks down. If you have a maintenance agreement, you just call for help and a representative will usually be there to lend a hand within an hour or two.

Procedures

Payment and Prepayment

I can't emphasize enough the value of getting prepayment. It will help avoid many hassles in the future. You may even wish to create prepayment forms. You can simply invoice clients and customers with the prepaid terms stated on your invoice. State the standard information, including title of book, list price, any discounts, net amount, and postage. Under terms, indicate *Prepayment Required*.

Even though you should try to get orders prepaid whenever possible, there will be times when you're going to have to send an invoice to a customer. However, before you agree to invoice, ask the customer to supply you with references. Also ask if they can fax the information to you so you can keep it on file.

If a customer uses a purchase order, always keep a copy of the original purchase order. Occasionally you may have trouble getting payment, and if the purchaser wants proof of having placed the order, you can provide a copy of their original order form.

Make sure to stay on top of your invoicing. It's easy to get behind, especially on collections, since it's an unpleasant duty. When you take an order on the telephone, make sure that you get the name of the person placing the order and keep your notes attached to the order blank. Keep copies of all invoices and purchase orders. They just may come in handy during a dispute.

If you can't keep up with your invoices, it may be time to consider hiring an accountant, bookkeeper, or CPA to help with your paperwork. One economical way is to advertise for a retired CPA or accountant who can handle small business books. A note of caution, however: make certain that anyone you're considering has kept up to date on current tax laws, because it can cost you dearly if you run afoul of the IRS. Other good sources of reasonably priced help are the Small Business Administration (SBA) and Service Corps of Retired Executives Association (SCORE). You may be able to find valuable help through those associations and SCORE provides free consulting services to small businesses and start-ups. You can find these organizations in the phone book or online at www.sba.gov and www.score.org.

Shipping

Another important aspect of your business will be shipping, including sending out galleys and review copies. Perhaps only fifty books will go out at any given time, but even that small quantity can quickly become a major headache.

Even though you may not send out shipments often, you'll need access to a service that offers Next Day Air or Second Day Air. The service will also need to be available when you need them—so all you have to do is pick up the phone and call. Research shipping providers in your own community, and remember that there are several national companies that you'll find useful as well.

I've found it valuable to set up a UPS (United Parcel Service) account, but FedEx is also a reliable carrier, as are DHL and Roadway. The USPS (United States Post Office) has made great strides in keeping up with the shipping business over the past couple decades. Check your Yellow Pages or go online and find out what kinds of services are offered and at what cost.

One benefit of using a company like UPS is that when you're shipping books, they're automatically insured up to $100 with no additional fee. If you're sending a shipment with more than $100 value, it can be insured for a higher amount for a nominal fee. UPS ships faster than the USPS media rate, too, so if time is of the essence (and it usually is), check into UPS or one of the other major package handlers.

You'll find UPS online at www.ups.com, FedEx at www.fedex.com, DHL at www.dhl.com, and Roadway at www.roadway.com.

Sometimes if you belong to certain organizations or associations (such as PMA and other publishing associations), you may be eligible for shipping discounts, as well. It never hurts to ask, and any money you save will improve your bottom line.

Make sure to clearly indicate the shipping costs on your order forms and fliers. The shape and size of the book will affect what you charge for shipping and handling. You may want to create a sliding scale for shipping charges, based upon the number of books ordered. Charge a certain amount for the first book and add increasingly smaller charges for larger quantities of the same book shipped to the same address.

When calculating your shipping charges, don't forget to include the cost of your supplies, such as padded envelopes, shipping labels, and boxes. For an 8?" x 11" book, I recommend using a box instead of a padded envelope. The odds of a book that size getting damaged are greater in an envelope than a box.

Freight Collect

In the past several years, I've begun to have a number of university bookstore accounts ask for their books to be shipped freight collect. When I first heard the term, I thought that freight collect meant that the purchaser would pay upon receipt of the books, like a COD (cash on delivery) account.

However, I quickly learned that freight collect means that

these companies have an account set up with vendors that deliver (such as UPS or Roadway) and when you send them books, you don't charge the buyer for shipping. Instead, you set up a special freight collect account first with the carrier, and the carrier bills bill the bookstore for the freight charges.

To help sell more books, you'll probably want to accept MasterCard, VISA, American Express, and Discover, but it takes a little know-how to set up the accounts. You'll find some helpful hints in some of Dan Poynter's brochures if you decide to accept credit card payments from your customers. Allowing your customers more payment options will make it easier for them to send you payments, thereby increasing your sales volume.

Filing System

Any business needs to be thoroughly organized and able to find documents or other information quickly. It isn't enough to say, "Oh, it's in the computer" when you need a billing statement or a copy of a press release. Back up hard copies of computer-generated material, particularly press releases, because safeguards can be welcome in a time of disaster, such as a computer meltdown.

Make sure your file names will make it easy to find something in a hurry, even if it's not an emergency situation. For instance, use a book's title as part of all files relating to that book, so you'll immediately know that a particular file has to do with a particular book.

Are we all in agreement?

III.

Expanding Your Business

Contracts

When you're first starting out, I recommend that you think long and hard before considering publishing books for other authors—but if you do, having a contract is of the utmost importance. Dan Poynter sells a publishing contract that can be of great assistance in getting started. It's a document you can add to or modify to suit your purposes.

If you're going to start publishing books, you'll want to hire an attorney who specializes in publishing to go over your contract. I've had many people tell me that they were very disappointed with their publisher's marketing and promotion efforts. Everything should be spelled out quite clearly in your contract so that both parties understand their obligations, rights, and duties.

When I agree to provide support services to a client, I adjust my marketing plan to that particular client's needs, wishes, and budget. I also do my best to make sure that we both understand all the conditions.

Recently, I heard of another professional's approach. When she's negotiating with a potential client, she asks that person to write out the terms of the contract. The client then writes the agreement and they both sign it. If there's a problem later on, the contract is in the client's own words, which makes it hard to argue that the client didn't understand the terms of the agreement. By letting them create the contract, all her clients know exactly what they've have agreed to.

If you want to consider publishing books by other people, contact the *Literary Market Place* about getting your company listed. You can be listed free if you publish more than three books a year. If not, you may have to pay to be listed as a small press publisher. Nevertheless, *LMP* is be a great resource, as is the *Writer's Market*, which has an application form you'll have to complete before you can be accepted for a listing.

Having listings in those two publications represents proof of your seriousness about being a publisher. In fact, there are some distributors who will base their acceptance of your business on those listings.

Paying for Talent

When you're publishing books for other authors, you'll have to face the question of whether a writer or an illustrator is doing work for hire or if that person should receive a percentage of the income or royalty payments.

Tricky Questions

Does an illustrator whose work consists of fifty percent or more of a children's book deserve a royalty? Probably, as opposed to someone who just does the cover art, for example.

Professional associations (such as artists guilds) often have guidelines and stipulations, but whatever your ultimate decision may be, always make sure that your contract or employment agreement is clearly understood by everyone concerned. Read sample contracts and, if necessary, have an attorney with experience in the publishing field review your contracts, especially when you're first beginning to publish books for other people. You can get attorney referrals from a local lawyer referral service, online, or from professional publishing organizations such as PMA (Publishers Marketing Association). You'll find more information in the Appendix.

Organizations/Associations for Networking

Just as professional organizations in other fields plan activities to allow contact between members, so do organizations in the publishing field. Those organizations range from local or state authors and publishers associations to national organizations, such as PMA. It's beneficial to belong to several associations, if only to have experienced professionals available who can understand what you're going through when you need to pick someone's brain.

These organizations also offer awards, workshops, speakers, and cooperative promotional programs. Many of them have newsletters that will welcome news of your activities and will announce new opportunities to their members.

I've networked through various organizations from the very beginning of my career. Recently, a woman called me about the co-opportunity marketing that I offer. During the course of our conversation, we exchanged information about distributors and our publishing experiences. I happened to mention that I was satisfied with Quality Books and Unique Books, and she told me of a reliable distributor she knew. She also gave me the names of several representatives in her part of the country who could help market one of my books to a specialized clientele.

Research Assistance

A valuable and economical source of assistance when you're first getting started in the business of self-publishing is the reference librarians at your local library. Just call them and explain your needs, and you'll find them eager to direct you to books, publications, and articles on whatever subject you require.

I've contacted my local library more times than I can count, asking them to do some research for me and then to fax me the information. They charge a small fee per page, but their information is always helpful and it saves me a trip to the library. They're generally fast, too, which means that I'm economizing on both time and gas when I ask for their help.

It also allows me to do other things while they're doing the research I've requested.

When you have questions, an important part of running any business is knowing who to call, where to call, when to call, and utilizing all available resources.

PART THREE

I. Publicity, Promotion, and Marketing

Publicity vs. Advertising
How to Get Free Publicity on Television by Jess Todtfeld
Basic Prepublication Materials
Prepublication Announcements
Galley Proofs
Press Release
Ordering Information
Media Kit
Reply Card
Flyers
Order Form

II. Media and Mailing Lists

Key Journals
Specialized Targets
Mailing List Sources
Mailing Lists for Follow-Ups
Merge Mailings
Ongoing Publicity
Awards
Book Signings
When Disaster Strikes, Strike Back! by Lynda Exley
Specialized Locales
Trade Shows and Conferences
Time-Geared Publicity
Getting the Books Out
Be Ever Alert
Creating Follow-Up
Writing Articles
Enhancing Your Business

Publicity, Promotion, and Marketing

Publicity vs. Advertising

Free publicity is far better advertising for your book than taking out a paid ad because publicity lends credibility and is, in essence, an endorsement—which can help you sell more books as a result. If your book is mentioned in a major magazine, it's human nature to expect orders to start pouring in. However, that's rarely the case. Free publicity is more about gaining credibility—for your book, for you as an author, and for your publishing business. Distributors are also more likely to take on a book that is being actively publicized and promoted, although that still doesn't mean that you're going to experience a significant jump in sales volume.

Advertising doesn't always guarantee immediate book sales, either—no more than advertising the grand opening any other business would. Whether people buy your book or not, you'll have to pay for any advertising you do.

There's an advertising adage that says people need to see an ad at least a dozen times before they'll take action, which means running ads can get expensive, but I know from personal experience that repetition—whether paid or unpaid—can pay off. Several years ago, Success magazine ran an article on me, which led to a guest spot on a radio talk show. After the radio show, someone called on my toll-free number and asked if I was the same person who'd been written about in Success. Apparently, her daughter had sent the Success article to her and then, after she heard me on the radio, she called to order a book—so I know that repetition can yield positive results.

People often ask me if having their books in the library will hurt sales, and I always answer with a definite, "Maybe, maybe not."

Not everyone can afford to buy every book that interests them, so if your main concern is getting the word out to as large an audience as possible, being in libraries can help you accomplish that goal, even if it means selling fewer books. However, it can work the other way, too. I've had many orders from people who initially saw one of my books in a library. In one case, a woman told me that she'd checked out *Nannies, Maids & More* so many times that she felt guilty and finally decided to buy her own copy. Would I have been able to reach that woman on my own? I doubt it—but I was able to reach her through her local library.

To market, to market...

How to Get Free Publicity on Television

Radio and television can make a major impact on your publicity efforts. Media interviews can be a great advertisement for your book, and best of all, they're free.
by Jess Todtfeld

Jess Todtfeld is president of Media Training Worldwide, a company that trains experts, authors, and business executives not only to look and perform better in front of the camera, but to leverage the power of the media. He is also a former TV producer, having worked on shows like *The O'Reilly Factor* with Bill O'Reilly. Jess explains how to get your message on the tube.

No one will argue if you say that television is a medium that exerts a powerful influence on people. Everyone knows that advertising financially supports the shows that we see on television. Advertisers aren't stupid; they wouldn't pay the big bucks if they didn't know that their ads have the power to influence millions of people. A message that comes through the television is stronger than one from billboards, magazines, radio, or any other medium. This is why you want your message to be on television.

The question remains, "How do I get television producers, the people between me and those cameras, to help me out?"

Don't Worry, Be Happy!

The first step is to acquire the right mind-set. By the right mind-set, I mean you should put away any anxieties you may have. Instead, use that energy to become excited about this new challenge and potential opportunity. Many people I train and work with get worried about this process. It's not as difficult as one might think.

Some get nervous at the prospect of calling up a busy producer to bother him or her about whatever it is they're trying to publicize. To ease the anxiety that might be associated with this, I'll tell you a few secrets that will make this seemingly arduous process a breeze. Hey, you've made it this far. You have something to promote. Not many people can say they had anything worthwhile to say or promote on television, so you should be proud of your accomplishment. Now it's time to take that accomplishment (and the new-found confidence that comes with it), transfer it to the most exciting medium there is, and get the results you're looking to achieve.

First off, the job of a TV producer is to come up with interesting ideas that they think viewers might want to see. Part of their job is hunting down these ideas so that their bosses think they're doing a good job. Your call is most likely helping them do their job.

What you have to do is pitch your idea for a segment on their show. You might think it strange to use a word like pitching in this circumstance. Usually we associate pitching with the creative process—for example, the script for a new movie or sit-com—but really, television news programs and talk shows work the same way. There are thousands of ideas for segments or shows. With so many to choose from or to research, producers want to select only those they think will make for interesting television. If you can make your pitch a persuasive one, you've just made this person's life a little bit easier. The more work you can do for producers through all parts of the process, the more it will benefit you in the long run.

Second, you'd be surprised at how young many of today's television producers are. Why am I telling you this? It can be calming to know that many of the professionals on the other end of the phone are half your age. It may give you the confidence you need to explain to them why their viewers would benefit from a segment done on you, your book, or your product.

Third, if you don't do it, no one will. It's better to try and fail than to have not tried at all. You can do nothing and get no publicity—or take your best shot.

I'll Scratch Your Back if You Scratch Mine!

Let's say that you're trying to publicize a book that you've written. Let's say that the topic is needlepoint. What you really want is to get the word out about your book so that people will buy it. What the television producer wants is *interesting programming*.

The question becomes, "How can everyone be happy and get what they want?"

It's simple. Put yourself in the shoes of the other person. If you were the producer of say, a local morning talk show, would you put an author on television whose pitch is: "I want everyone to know that I have a new book about needlepoint?" No. Right off, it sounds boring. If you were the producer, you'd want to find the most interesting topic for your show. It's your job as your own publicist to convince the producer that you're the ticket to interesting television, so be creative in pitching your idea.

A better pitch might be: "How about a segment on a stress-reducing pastime that more Americans are discovering every day?" Or you could try: "What is it about needlepoint that's attracting Generation X?"

Already the producer's brain can start to envision how this segment will develop into something the average viewer will stay tuned to see. Needlepoint is a perfect example of a tough sell. It may not appeal to everyone, but if you find the right angle, you can give it universal appeal. You just have to be creative.

How Do I Pitch a Strike of an Idea?

To get your point across to a producer, you must prepare to pitch your idea. This isn't a difficult process. It's really just a telephone call or email telling them that you have an idea for their show, but you'll have to prepare first. The following is a list of things you should do to get off on the right foot with a prospective producer:

- Write a pitch letter. Whether you're pitching a book you authored, a product you made, or just yourself as an expert, you'll need to have a pitch letter prepared. Make it simple and to the point. Many producers will just skim it, if they read it at all. Use bulleted points or large text to highlight important points you want to make.

- Think of angles. As I mentioned earlier, you need to do as much work as you can for the producer. Think of the various ways the producer could do a segment on your idea. Be creative, especially if it's an unusual or seemingly uninteresting topic for television. Thought over long enough, anything can be made interesting to the average viewer.

- Prepare materials for emailing or snail mailing. (No faxes. That's so 1988.) Now that you know what you're going to say, put it on paper. Don't let this part slow you down. Don't spend hours or days laboring over each word you write. Like I said, most producers will only skim the information. If you can write a separate sheet outlining a biography (bio) of yourself, make that a part of your materials. If you have or decide to write a sheet or two that goes into extended detail on whatever it is that you're hoping to promote, also make that a part of the materials. When you're all done, you'll have a press kit. Remember, less is usually more, and you're really trying to make sure the most basic questions are answered: who, what, when, where, why, and how.

- If it's a physical mailing, include the product. If it's a book, CD, or product you're trying to promote, be prepared to send whatever it is along with all of your other press information. Producers will need to see something tangible to be read, tried out, or sampled. Although you have to plan on giving a lot of your work away, never to be returned to you, sending it is crucial. All publicists do this. Because you're acting as your own publicist, you need to be seen in the same professional light if you want to be taken seriously.

Where Art Thou, Program?

Now that you've prepared your press materials, you're ready to make your contacts. What you'll need to do is make a list of where you'll go with your pitch. Think about the outlets you'll want to pitch yourself to. Make a list of the television stations in your area. Then make a list of national television shows that you think you'd be right for. Making a good match is a big part of it. You wouldn't pitch *This Old House* a segment story idea on a new book you've written titled *The Truth About President Harry S. Truman*.

Check the Yellow Pages to get the numbers of the television stations in your area. Some may have websites where you can find out about the various shows a channel offers. Call the stations and ask for a segment producer or booker on that show.

If you're considering calling a national show, there are a couple of things to keep in mind. Producers of national shows will usually prefer an in studio guest over one via satellite from another city. Think about where you are in relation to where they are. Many of the national morning talk shows are located in New York. Would it sway them if you planned a trip to New York? These are bargaining points that you need to think about and consider.

If hunting down producer phone numbers is a part of the process you'd be happy to bypass, you can always buy a list.

Ring-a-Ling!

Making phone calls is probably the most crucial part of the process (even in the age of email). Without phone calls, most of your work will be done in vain. This is how you start the process off—and how you end it. This is the way a producer gets a sense of who you are.

Don't be afraid. You never know whom you're dealing with on the other end. You may get someone who is nice and genuinely interested in what you have to say or you may get a cold and uninterested person who will dismiss you and your segment idea in a heartbeat. Either way, without a phone call, your pitch letter has a good chance of ending up in the physical or electronic recycle bin, and the product you've sent along with it will end up in the trash or collecting dust underneath a desk. That's why I suggest making an initial interest call to find out if you should even send the material you've put together.

To help guide you through the call, you have your pitch letter, which you've spent lots of time thinking about. Try to be short and to the point. Let the producer know that you think you have an interesting segment idea for the show and be prepared to follow up the conversation with a fax or mailing of more information. Follow up with another call to see if there's continued interest. Don't worry about bothering the producer. Unless you're calling more than three times a week, you're not a bother. You're just someone who is interested in getting on the show. Most producers understand that. Listen to the tone in their voice. You'll know if they feel you're calling them too much. Many times, producers are thankful for the reminder.

Attention Seekers

Do your research. I'm not saying that you need to spend hours, days, weeks, or months researching possible outlets for publicity. The most important thing you need to know is who it is that you're pitching. By who, I mean the particular style and content of any given program. I can't tell you how many people used to call me with no idea what kind of program I worked on. If you watch a show for five minutes, you'll know that a new spongy toy you've designed to turn colors in the bath may not be the best topic for a political debate show or a cooking program. This is obviously a ridiculous example, but the point is clear. It's important to have done some homework if you want your pitch to be taken seriously. Also, you'll be saving yourself a great deal of time in the long run. Like most people pitching ideas and, with any luck, appearing on television, you have a full-time job to do and don't need to waste your time on fruitless phone calls.

You'll impress the producer if you say something about either the program or the program's host(s). That shows that you've taken enough interest to watch. A little schmoozing never hurts. In fact, if the producer can be warmed up, you greatly increase the chances that he or she will truly listen to your pitch.

If you've already received some publicity—say, a newspaper article—use it in your pursuit for more publicity. Send a copy along with your pitch letter to a producer. It will give you more credibility. It shows the producer that someone else thought that you were interesting, and they should, too.

It should be noted that some print and television outlets carry more weight than others. If you boast about being written up by the local *Pennysaver*, it won't do as much for you as an article in *USA Today*. The same goes for television. If you've been interviewed on *Oprah* and *The Today Show*, play it up. Use it to help get you on other shows. Saying that you did an hour on the local cable-access channel will most likely not impress a producer.

There are ways, however, to get around this. If you have an article that was written by a small paper, cut out the article by itself. If it's from the local *Pennysaver*, cut the name of the newspaper off the sheet. If it's a small, yet respected paper, keep the name on the page in one spot or write it in. If you made an appearance on a small television show and are proud of your performance, offer the tape only if you think it will help get you booked on a show. Make sure to let the people you're sending it to know what to expect before they see it. Poor production values could end up making you look bad.

Don't Sweat the Setbacks

Just as in any other part of life, there will be setbacks in this process. You'll probably at some point encounter a producer with a bad attitude, you may deal with someone who says they're interested but isn't, or you'll receive rejection. Just know that it's part of the process. My only advice is to do your best to be diplomatic and polite while talking to producers on the phone. Keep making the effort. Another producer may put you on a show, which might lead to a newspaper article, which might lead to a booking on a show by a producer who wouldn't give you the time of day before.

What do you do if you leave a message for a producer and they don't call you back? This can be frustrating. They might not have returned your call because they became very busy for a few days and just forgot. Call them back and try to connect with that person. Don't give up until they've told you themselves that this isn't something they want to do.

Tommy, Can You Hear Me?

It should be no surprise to you that what you say and how you say it conveys a lot of information to a producer. Talking with someone on the phone and talking with that same person in person is quite different. Think of a telemarketer's job. It's an extreme challenge to get a stranger to buy something over the phone. A telemarketer isn't a face or a person to the people on the other end of the line. A telemarketer is just a voice, so the process is impersonal. You're like a telemarketer. You're on the phone, talking to somebody who doesn't know you, to make a pitch to sell your idea. Especially when you don't know the person, connecting with them can seem difficult and grabbing their attention a challenge.

Without a doubt, you'll be dismissed if, out of nervousness, you:

- Have trouble putting sentences together well.
- Have difficulty elaborating on whatever you're trying to promote or talk about on television.
- Talk too softly or too loudly.
- Go off on strange tangents that make it hard for the producer to follow what you're saying.
- Read verbatim from your press information.
- Sound like a low-energy person.

If you exhibit any of these characteristics or any other awkwardness or signs of social ineptness, you'll scare a producer and most likely won't appear on the show. For example, if you come off as someone with low energy, the producer likely will think that you'll appear that way on the air. The producer can't take any risks. The people booked on the show reflect how good, or in this case how bad, that person is at finding interesting guests for interesting segments.

My last suggestion on this front: get media training before pitching your book. Most authors wait until they get a big interview and then scramble to find someone who can make them come across the right way. Take part in a media training workshop or private session where you're physically selling yourself or product in an interview setting. This will actually make you better at the pitch process. Your pitch will sound like an interview, and the media will be happy that they got what they expected.

Help, I Need Somebody!

At this point, you might be thinking, "Should I get a publicist?"

Appearing on television is important to you, and you don't want to do something that will keep you from getting what you want.

You may ask yourself, "What if I don't have the right energy on the phone?"

Well, you don't need a publicist to get yourself on television. Of course, it doesn't hurt, but that's not why you bought this book. If you come to a telephone conversation fully prepared, if you're confident, and if you've prepared by putting yourself in the producer's position to try to find out what they want, you'll be okay. Once you've done these things, you'll increase your chances of landing a spot on the producer's show, where you'll have exposure to a large number of people. After getting on that first show, you will have gained the credibility you'll need to get booked for other television interviews. It only gets easier from that point. You'll become experienced and learn something from each interview you do.

What should you do if you're bumped or canceled from a show? Try to find out why you were taken off the show. Do everything you can to get yourself booked again, short of being a pest. Be as flexible as possible. If a producer took the time and energy to book you the first time, it was because that person thought you were worthy of being on the show. You most likely were bumped or canceled due to reasons beyond the producer's control.

Hi, Mom, I'm on TV!

Let's say that you made the connection. A producer wants you to come on and talk about your area of expertise. You aren't bumped or canceled from the show. You figure that you'll mark the day on your calendar, show up, answer a few questions, walk away, and viewers at home will respond to what you say. It sounds simple enough, but it's not quite that easy.

You Look Mahhhhvelous!

What does being a good guest mean? If all goes well, being a good guest means that you'll be someone who will be called again. You'll be someone who is recommended to other producers by the person who booked you. And many times, being a good guest means that you were able to get your point through to the viewer. Before you appear for your interview, you should prepare some objectives for yourself that are clear. This way you'll have some guidelines to say everything you want to say. (Many times you won't end up covering it all, but it's good to have a game plan.)

On many shows, the producer will call you up a couple of days (or sometimes a couple of weeks) before the interview to confirm everything with you and may also do what's called a pre-interview. In this pre-interview, the producer will prepare you by asking questions that will be similar to the host's questions. This isn't always done, but if it is done, two reasons for doing it are: 1) The producer can get a better idea of how you will respond on television, and 2) it will give you an idea of what will happen during the segment. Often, however, a pre-interview is in the form of a casual conversation between you and the producer.

Don't worry if you're not given a pre-interview (and don't subsequently bother the producer for one). You'll be informed before the show of how the segment will go and what will be expected from you. The best preparation you can do is by yourself. If you need to, go back over all of your press information. This will help highlight the important points in the interview.

You definitely don't want to be labeled as a needy guest. One of the biggest pitfalls is becoming an overeager or needy guest. You could end up shooting yourself in the foot. If this is your first time being interviewed, great. Don't think that just because you've been booked on the show that your new friend, the producer, can speak to you constantly about every worry and concern. If you have questions, jot them down and try to ask them all at once. High-maintenance guests are the first ones who find themselves cut on a busy day or end up getting their air time shortened. Be confident. You got this far, so you'll be fine.

Here are a few other things you should keep in mind to ensure that this interview won't be your last. If you follow these tips, you'll ensure a successful appearance and will increase your chances of being called to appear again. You will, at the very least, have a good tape of your fine interview that you can show to future producers.

- Be on time to the studio.
- Match your style of clothing to the style of the show.
- Look well-groomed.
- Be a high-energy guest.
- Act friendly and cooperate with the host(s).
- Elaborate fully—don't give one-word responses.
- Use short anecdotes to illustrate ideas.

Get a Hold of Those Reins!

During the interview, it's all about control. Many people think that an interview is a meeting between people where one asks questions and the other gives answers. Even though it's the job of the television anchor or host to lead you through the interview, it's important to take some of the control. One person is asking questions, but you must have a roadmap with your answers laid out along the way. It's important to think about where everyone is coming from when they meet in an interview situation.

We've established that you're there because you want to get a message across. Ultimately, you either want people to buy your book, product, or service, or you want to persuade the wider audience to agree with you on some particular topic you've been brought on to discuss.

The interviewer is sitting down to do one of thousands of interviews. Who knows how much preparation that person has done this day? The interviewer might not have done any.

Don't just sit there and answer questions. A good guest is always thinking about the big picture. Just like a good politician, you need to come to the table with an agenda and an idea of what you want to say. Just because you weren't asked a specific question that would allow you to make a point, that doesn't mean you can't bring that point up. You should be cooperative enough to answer any question the interviewer asks, but you can also redirect the flow of conversation to allow you to make the points you want to make.

Practice at home if you need to. Find out how much time you'll be getting for the interview. The average would be from three to six minutes. That may seem short to you, but to the people who are at home with their remote controls, it's a very long time. Do what you can to get enough of your points across to entice viewers to find out more about you.

What do you do if you were told that you'd get six minutes of air time and you only get three? The answer: deal with it. You should be happy to get the opportunity to be on television for a little self-promotion. Make the most out of the three minutes you get. Give some great information and leave the viewers wanting more. You might end up with a better segment.

What if you're promised six minutes and you only get thirty seconds? Practice getting your most important message points into one full answer. I teach people the art of mastering this skill during media training sessions. I've had clients who've been in this exact situation. If they get all their top points in, they've still accomplished their goal and can walk away from an interview knowing they said everything they wanted to get into the interview.

Could You Mention That 101 More Times?

"Watch me hold up my book while I answer your question and say, 'Gee, that's something that I cover in chapter two of my new book!'"

If you want a television interview to be your last, you'll become an overzealous promoter. Every television producer expects you to throw your plug in, but exercise a little restraint. There's nothing worse than a guest who has to drop their plug into every answer they give. You may think that it will help viewers remember who you are, but the result will be to anger those who've given you the opportunity to be on television, and to give viewers the feeling that you're trying to sell them something instead of giving them information. Selling is for commercials, not television shows (even though you're obviously there to promote your product).

Just try to remember that the producer wants you there to make for an interesting segment for the program's viewers. You don't need to do shameless plugging. It's standard for an interviewer to mention your plug at the beginning—or at least at the end—of the interview. In addition, it will be listed on the screen below your name to let viewers know who you are.

There are ways to seamlessly work your plug into the conversation.

One guest might say, "I did a study for the book, which found—"

Viewers are then saying to themselves, "Hmm, that's

interesting. What book did this person write?"

This technique is something you'll have to work on. I recommend doing it only a couple of times during the interview, and in the most subtle way you can. This is a very important technique for turning interviews into sales.

By the way, that's the point of doing interviews. People get sidetracked with everything that precedes an interview and forget that they're there to sell something.

Robert Kiyosaki, bestselling author of *Rich Dad, Poor Dad*, says, "They don't call it a best-written book. They call it a bestselling book."

One Good Hand Returns Another

I talked a little bit about how being a good guest will help you in the long run. You'd be surprised how the media plays off one another. Many television producers get their ideas from newspaper articles, and many newspaper writers watch television for ideas. Do your best to get as much information out there as you can. Try to make it interesting. If you can make it sound interesting to your friends and family, you'll be able to make it interesting for viewers and those who might want to book you on another show.

That's All, Folks

The best advice I can give? Don't worry and don't stress. If you think you have something people will want to hear about and if you truly believe it's interesting, the people you talk to will also. As long as you do the preparatory work outlined here, you'll shine under those studio lights. Don't forget to enjoy the process. Good luck!

For more tips, send me an email at JessResources@MediaTrainingWorldwide.com or check out www.AuthorMediaResources.com.

Basic Prepublication Materials

At times you may feel that your book itself is the least of the printed materials you'll need, and in some ways you'll be right. Without prepublication materials, your book will just be floating somewhere out in the wind.

Prepublication Announcements

Immediately after you've settled on a title for your book, its subject matter, and your publishing company's name, get your book listed in R.R. Bowker's *Books in Print*. It's the standard reference source for every book's title, author, and publisher. In fact, it's gotten so comprehensive that it's been split into several specific volumes, including one called *Forthcoming Books* and others cataloged by subject, author, and title. You can find out what information Bowker requires by visiting their website at www.bowker.com.

Galley Proofs

Sending out galleys will be one of your most important prepublication activities. Galleys should be sent according to the guidelines of each particular publication, but many of them require galleys ninety days prior to the publishing release date. Some publications will review only the galley proof stage, while others will review only in finished form. For help, refer to Dan Poynter's publications or to *Literary Market Place*.

Press Release

Time your press release to either coincide with your book's publication date or to slightly precede it and send it to as many appropriate publications as you can afford. The ideal press release is both an announcement and a pitch letter. It's meant to evoke excitement and curiosity about your book while prompting a desire to know more about it. Your press release should also include details on how to obtain copies, whether from a bookstore, a distributor, or from you personally. It should also include brief information about you as the author and your credentials.

Ordering Information

I discovered early on that when I sent out publicity, some reviews and interviews would include my company's name, but many didn't tell people how to buy their own copies. If potential buyers can't reach you, the publicity you've gained won't help sell more books, especially if your book isn't available in major bookstore chains. So make sure that ordering information is given whenever you can.

I create a cover sheet to send out with my press releases that urges reviewers to include ordering information with any mention of my books. If you don't ask, you may be wasting a golden opportunity for free publicity—and increased sales. Some publications have policies against giving out ordering information, but even those publications may have no problem with at least giving out your company name and where your office is located. It's not perfect, but it's better than nothing, since people who are interested in your book can still find you through sources such as the Internet, *Literary Market Place* or *Books in Print*.

Media Kit

A media kit is every bit as important as your press release. You'll find many uses for media kits. You can use it to reply to inquiries for radio or TV appearances, to give away at book signings, as a distributor sales tool, and to accompany submissions to contests.

A media kit should contain background on your book, a reproducible photo of the book, and a photograph and biographical information about yourself. If your book has received complimentary comments or impressive reviews, include those, too, as well as information about any honors and awards you've received. Add new information to your media kit as it becomes available, since you may use revised versions of your media kit for years.

Reply Card

Always include an acknowledgement card in your media kits and press releases. The card should indicate a place to acknowledge receipt of the book, whether the recipient plans to review it, the date the review will appear, and if the reviewer needs any additional material. Not everyone will return the card, but it's good to know when someone is planning to review your book, and the card provides an easy way to ask for additional information.

Some recipients may want another photograph or some line illustrations. Your reply card can either be postage paid or have to place to put a stamp. It's more economical to let the recipient pay the postage, but if you have a postal permit for business mailings, that permit can be used on the cards—and you'll get more replies.

Another good way to get replies and requests for more information quickly is to include your company's email information and website address on your reply card.

Flyers

You'll find many uses for flyers, and they should be one of the first pieces of promotional material you create. Like a press release, a flyer is also a pitch letter, but it must also give pertinent information about your book.

An eye-catching design is vital. The first rule: Keep it simple. Always include:
The title of your book
A picture of your book
A synopsis of your book's content
Information about yourself

Order Form

The biggest challenge when preparing a flyer is to keep it simple. Every book has a great deal that could be said about it, but the person receiving your flyer often won't read it if it contains too much information. Therefore, most flyers are printed on only one side of the paper, but two-sided fliers can sometimes be effective, too, like the flyer for *Productive Bankers, Profitable Banks* in the Appendix.

Cards can be economical and eye-catching flyers, particularly if they're mailed separately. The recipient will get your message at a glance, they cost less to mail, and they don't require envelopes, thereby saving on supply costs. You also generally don't have to include dates on your book flyers, which means they can used as follow-up information and for newly discovered promotional areas.

Friends and Family
do not a mailing
list make.

II.

Media and Mailing Lists

$\bullet$

Key Journals

One of the primary keys to promotion, publicity, and sales of your book will be getting it reviewed in appropriate influential journals, including basic book-related publications like the ones listed below. (Full addresses are given in the Appendix):

Booklist
Kirkus Reviews
Library Journal
New York Times Review of Books
Publishers Weekly
School Library Journal

Besides these mainstays, you'll want to get in touch with any specialized publications in your field and try to get a review in their publication. There's no better review than a favorable one that's read by the very people who will be most interested in your book. You can do online searches for potential review sites and publications by typing a couple relevant key words into your browser.

If you decide to purchase a mailing list of book reviewers, make certain it's current and consists of relevant reviewers in major markets. You can economize by simply sitting down and doing an exhaustive Internet search, since a great deal of the information you'll need will be available on the World

Wide Web. The trick is locating that information and then taking the time to research each potential reviewing source carefully, including finding out their requirements for submitting books for review. There's no use sending information about an art book to a sports publication (unless it happens to be an art book featuring some form of sport) or news about an imaginative children's book to a business publication. *Literary Market Place, Gale's Directory of Publications,* and *Broadcast Media* all categorize various media according to fields of interest.

Don't overlook book clubs, gift sales, organization newsletters, award sponsors, and book catalog publishers, either. Your object should be to get your book favorably reviewed as many times as possible by as many different reviewers as possible.

You'll find lots of suggestions for John Kremer's *1001 Ways to Market Your Book,* Dan Poynter's books, and many others. Just type in key words such as book marketing and book promotion into your browser and then start researching the thousands of opportunities that will be available for you to reach your target audience.

Specialized Targets

You'll also find unique opportunities to explore in your own local area. Every region of the country has book reviewers in newspapers and magazines, as well as local radio and TV talk shows that feature writers, artists, and musicians on a regular basis. You can generally get your schedule of book signings, lectures, readings, and other events listed on local websites and in publications.

Include a select number of leaders or policy makers in the field to receive copies of your book. If your book is about art, for example, you might send copies to local art instructors or the heads of art departments in local schools and colleges, who might then recommend your book to their classes.

Mailing List Sources

If you decide to buy a mailing list, make sure it's current and specializes in the types of publications that will help generate sales of your book. We use Cision for our list of media outlets. Their list is kept current, but the fees may be prohibitive for small presses, at least in the beginning. You might to consider sharing an account with other small press publishers—if the company gives you the OK to do so.

The same is true for media outlets of all sorts. Purchase a current list of radio talk shows that either use a variety of authors or direct their efforts toward reaching your specific target audience. In every case, your marketing efforts must not only be economical, but they must also be effective.

You can buy mailing list databases that will also allow you to print out mailing labels as you need them and keep a record of the places you've contacted. Being able to print labels is a good idea, even if you compile your own personalized database while you're doing your Internet research. Printing labels on your computer can save time and energy that will be better used to explore new reviewing opportunities. Make sure to back up your database on a hard copy in case of a computer meltdown. Keep detailed records of your contacts and the outcome of those contacts.

Unless your book is quite specialized, you may want to target high circulation publications. However, nearly every book fits into some sort of interest category, so you may do just as well or better by targeting smaller publications that cater to readers with an interest in the field your book covers. Reaching one person with a passion for your book's subject matter is worth dozens of general interest readers who aren't. Another advantage to the smaller publications is that they're more likely to review your book. After all, if it's of interest to their readership, they want to tell those readers about it. To specialized publications, your book may actually be newsworthy, rather than just filler material—which is what it often would be to a large general interest publication.

When you're compiling your own list, get fax numbers,

telephone numbers, and email addresses of the appropriate people. If you can't find the exact person, you can send inquiries in care of a departmental editor, such as the sports editor or the food editor.

Mailing Lists for Follow-Ups

You'll also want to create a database of people who purchased your book. In one of my publications, I offered purchasers a free newsletter if they completed an enclosed postcard and returned it to my office. Many of those who responded had received the book as a company benefit, so I especially wanted their names and addresses. I received a number of postcards and used them for a follow-up mailing.

On the postcard there's a place for returnees to say how they heard about your book. If you include some type of questionnaire in your book, you'll get even more clues as to what people want and how they found your book in the first place.

I offered a free newsletter, but you might want to provide some sort of service you could offer at a discount. Such cards should be returned postpaid by using your business reply permit. You'll constantly be analyzing what works best and what doesn't work well.

Merge Mailings

However you prepare your mailing list, it can be used for merge mailings. If you purchase a database, you'll be able to merge the database with form letters as needed. It's easy to learn how to do. I even created my invoice pieces by using a database.

Ongoing Publicity

When thinking about publicity, you have to look beyond the first year. Look at McDonald's and Burger King. They've been around a long time, but hardly a day goes by that you don't see those companies advertising and promoting their businesses.

A client recently asked me how much time he should devote to promoting and marketing his book. I told him that I market and publicize one or another of my books every single day. If I stop promoting for just one week, I'll feel the effects a year down the road. Make no mistake: promoting and marketing should be an ongoing effort, whether you have one book or ten.

Awards

Always be on the lookout for new publicity opportunities—including awards, which can add credibility but won't necessarily result in book sales. The first year your book is out, it's new and newsworthy. However, if your book wins an award in its second year, it's newsworthy all over again and you'll have reason to celebrate. Winning an award will bring your book back into the spotlight, regardless of how long it may have been in print, so don't overlook contests. They can provide valuable publicity opportunities, which can lead to increased sales. *Literary Market Place* offers a list of organizations that sponsor such awards.

As a self-publisher, you're constantly striving for recognition and credibility, and awards can bring both. If your book wins an award, put a sticker on the front cover proclaiming that fact. It will bring additional attention to your book wherever it's displayed. It lends credibility to who you are and what you're doing, both of which can help generate more sales.

I have various award stickers that can be printed to show the name of the award a book has received. On the front of a book, stickers are visible and compelling to potential buyers in a bookstore. You only have about eight seconds to win over a customer, and an award sticker can give you an edge in attracting that customer's attention. Contact Five Star Publications and request a free label and rubber stamp catalog.

How can you find out about awards? The Publishers Marketing Association (PMA) offers many different kinds. For instance, if you've reprinted your book and it looks better than it did, PMA has an award for that. It also has awards for cover design and content. Those awards are one good reason to join PMA. *Literary Market Place* is a comprehensive source for finding out about the names and requirements of awards and contests. All you have to do is scan their listings and choose the contests that best fit your book.

Will an award sell more books? Not necessarily, but it can't hurt, and if nothing else, it will help heighten your credibility as a publisher. Winning an award also provides new chances to publicize your book, since winning the award is newsworthy. It could make the difference between getting the attention of a reviewer or being passed by. If an award generates a request for a review copy, it was worth the effort.

Book Signings

Book signings can generate promotional opportunities and will be newsworthy at any time. Just send out your schedule information to the calendar editors of the various publications in your area. Make sure to pay special attention to their deadlines. Often they're two to three weeks ahead of the event.

Major bookstores will often help with publicity about book signings, but never rely completely on that. Make your own list of agreed-upon duties and contact the bookstore to see if they've done what they said they would. Book signings can be as imaginative as you and the bookstore wish. In fact, doing something unusual will add to the promotional appeal and can tie in with other ways to promote your book.

For instance, I was asked to do a book signing for my cookbook *That Hungarian's in My Kitchen*. Since I'd compiled favorite recipes from my mother and my aunts, we were able to enlarge the book signing to include a food tasting. I also had some aprons made in both child and adult sizes that featured the book's front cover design. We displayed the aprons on easels at the bookstore. I had a promotional card printed that showed a drawing of the aprons as well as the book, and the aprons could be ordered separately. By including the aprons in my marketing efforts, I was often able to call book reviewers who had reviewed the book and mention the matching aprons.

A flyer designed for the author signing, recipe tasting event, including a sketch of the aprons, all designed to further interest in the book.

A word of caution about book signings. The location of the bookstore in terms of traffic is essential. I've done book signings in bookstores with very low traffic and they weren't as successful. Signings in stores that have heavy traffic on their own, however, will generally bring greater success, even if you're unknown. Your signing will get a lot of attention just because it's in a bookstore where there's lots of traffic.

Timing is also important. If possible, tie the signing to a newsworthy event or occasion. Holidays are popular times for publishers to try to get their authors into bookstores. The key is plan ahead and take advantage of all the help a store can provide.

Many stores are interested in promoting local authors. Occasionally a local authors' association may cooperate with a shopping mall for a *Meet Our Authors Day* or something similar. The mall provides tables where authors can display their books and talk to the customers—which is another good reason for being a member of your local writers association and for being known as a local publisher.

When Disaster Strikes, Strike Back!

Navigating the Book Circuit with a Twelve-Year-Old Author
by Lynda Exley

Believe it or not, there is such a thing as giving your audience too much of a good thing when it comes to marketing a children's book. How do I know this? The story begins with experiencing every writer's worst nightmare.

The biggest buzzword in book marketing these days is platform. You read it in blogs, books, and magazine articles, and hear it from lecturers in classrooms or during writers group meetings: "Authors must have creative platforms in order to effectively pitch their books."

With this in mind, my twelve-year-old son and I developed what we like to call our dog and pony show to sell his witty picture book, The Student from *Zombie Island: Conquering the Rumor Monster*, in bookstores. Our platform was to razzle dazzle children during story time. We would start out with a puppet show that humorously discussed rumors, followed by his reading of the book and ending with a children's craft that would keep the kiddies busy while their parents flocked to our table to purchase multiple copies of the book.

After a month of begging large bookstore chains to host us, we finally got several lined up. The bookstores' public relations coordinators loved the idea of having us give their store clerks a break by handling story time for them—and selling a few books while we were at it, too.

Our first three presentations were to be held over a four-day period at three different outlets of the same bookstore chain. Two days before show time, disaster struck.

The staff at the first bookstore on our agenda had no idea we were supposed to be there. I learned that when I called to notify them that we would be arriving an hour early to set up the puppet stage. That meant no in-store promotion, no books in stock, and no dog and pony show, since the children's area was already booked with other events.

After a flurry of phone calls between the bookstore manager, the corporate manager in charge of booking and marketing events, our publisher, and I, we agreed to bring books from my personal stock and sign them at a table near the front door. So much for a platform!

Experts will tell you there's nothing that turns customers off faster than a bored author sitting behind a table trying to hock his wares, so we had to think of something that would get people's attention fast—especially since none of the patrons would be expecting us.

As I set my right brain hemisphere into creative motion, thinking of how to make the best of the situation, my left brain decided it would be prudent to call the other two bookstores to see if they were in the same boat. As it turned out, the second bookstore knew we were coming but couldn't get the books in time and the third bookstore had the books on order and was certain they'd come in on time, but didn't know about the puppet show and craft.

Damage Control

The first order of business was to get some in-store publicity going, so I delivered books and bookmarks for a display and each store agreed to slap up a few flyers. Stores two and three had a few days to mention our event during other regularly scheduled story times and we even managed to get a few late notices into the calendar sections of local newspapers.

However, the situation with store number one was most perplexing, since another day had escaped during our panicked negotiations, leaving only one day to come up with a plan. A one-day in-store promotion wasn't going to draw enough people, so we had to think of something that would lure unsuspecting customers to our table.

"Who are our customers?" I asked myself.

They're parents and children.

"How can we attract the parents, who hold the purse strings, to us?"

By getting the attention of their children.

"And how do we do that?"

By providing something inexpensive that every child loves.

"And what would that be?"

Well, since I didn't know how to do face paint, I decided on balloons. Every child loves helium-filled balloons, and I could punch holes in the bookmarks and tie them to the opposite end of the balloon ribbon.

It worked like a charm. With a huge, disarming smile, my son greeted every child who walked into the door with a balloon and gave each parent an additional bookmark, explaining that it contained info for the book he wrote. It was exciting to see children's eyes light up at the sight of colorful balloons and watch them clutching the bookmarks at the end of the ribbons as their parents talked to my son about his book.

The balloons also created a stir with other families who entered by way of the café instead of the front entrance. With apparent envy, the kids asked where the other children had gotten their balloons. When they learned it was from the boy with the book, they eagerly approached our table to get their own balloons.

As one might expect, some children accidentally let go of their balloons, and by the end of the day, it was a Student from *Zombie Island* fantasy to see a dozen balloons with bookmarks hovering around the ceiling, advertising my son's book to anyone who looked up. We sold more than a dozen books and made as many contacts for school visits and other book promotion ventures.

Lessons on the Fly

Here's where the part about giving the audience too much of a good thing comes into the story. With the success we experienced at the first store on our book tour, even though it was a store that didn't know we were coming, had no books ordered, did no advertising, and hadn't given us an opportunity to do our puppet show, we were certain that we'd make an even bigger splash with our dog and pony show at the next two stores.

With great expectation, we set up our stage and readied our puppet-making craft for store number two. More than two dozen children filed in for our visit. Our puppet show, book reading, and craft went off without a hitch. In fact, the children asked us to read the book again while they used their own puppets to mouth the words as my son read The Student from *Zombie Island*. Ah, the glory of it all!

The kids had a great time and the parents and preschool teachers thanked us repeatedly for entertaining their children. My son manned his book signing table, ready with pen in hand, eagerly waiting to sign dozens of books for everyone who had so thoroughly enjoyed our story hour.

As everyone filed past him, gleefully playing with their puppets while exiting the children's area, my son's smile began to fade. Not one person bought a book.

What went wrong? Was it because most were preschool children accompanied by teachers rather than by their parents? That wouldn't be the case when we hit store number three, since the engagement was on a Saturday.

While pondering that, I asked the store manager to move our table out of the children's area, which was in the very back of the store. She agreed to move it up front, as it had been at store number one. On a hunch, I brought the helium and balloons, and we proceeded to meet and greet people as before. Again we sold a decent number of books.

With huge hopes, we set up our equipment and readied ourselves for the last store on our tour. This time our audience was all families. Surely it would be the great success we were anticipating.

Again the puppet show, book reading, and craft were a tremendous hit. Again parents and children thanked us over and over, and again we didn't sell a single book.

That's when it struck me that we'd given them too much of a good thing. We had given the children a great deal of entertainment, thus lifting their parents' guilt for purchasing a book for themselves, but not one for their children.

As one mother replied to her child who begged for a

book, "No, honey, you got to hear stories and make puppets, now it's Mom's turn to get something."

So what did we learn from all this?

For starters, less is sometimes more. The idea of giving balloons away was spurred by a damage control mentality, but that simple notion turned out to be our greatest draw for sales. Give your customers a little something to lure them over, providing yourself the opportunity to bend their ears and make a sale, instead of giving them so much that they feel satisfied without taking a second look at your book.

Do your part. I now call bookstores three weeks early to make sure they're aware of our upcoming visit and have books on order. At the same time, I send them a flyer to help them advertise our visit to their stores and bookmarks to use with displays. Furthermore, I send a suggested news release for them to send to the media. The news release will not only make their jobs easier, but will also serve as a polite reminder to advertise our event in a timely manner.

Finally, when a disaster derails your book tour, enjoy the ride. You just might learn something along the way—or end up traveling to a better place than originally planned.

And, always do whatever it takes to get your book signing table near the bookstore's main entrance.

Specialized Locales

Your book has to be seen as well as reviewed and described. Bookstores are one locale for the physical display of your book, but there are many other ways and places to get your book into public view. Many will depend on your resourcefulness and the type of book. Imagine a simple example, such as a new art book. Art galleries and museums would be two obvious places. If an art gallery agrees to take the book, you might want to follow up with a book signing and perhaps a wine and cheese tasting party and reception. Remember, however, even though a gallery may say it will do all the promotional work and publicity, you should still be involved. Even if your budget is limited, that doesn't necessarily mean you can't hire a publicist. Any professional help you can get along the way is wonderful.

If nothing else, you could create a press release for the area where the gallery is located and then develop a specialized media kit. If the gallery indicates that it will handle all the media, you should still provide all the necessary information. A publicity packet makes your book more saleable. If your book is accepted by several different galleries, it would be simple to revise your press release for each of them.

Trade Shows and Conferences

Make sure your book is included in displays at appropriate conferences. PMA provides opportunities for having books on display, as do Five Star Publications, the American Book Association (ABA), and the American Library Association (ALA). Once you've done one display, it won't be long before you'll begin receiving literature from other companies asking you to participate in theirs.

Some of them do nothing but book displays and charge per book. The fees will range depending upon the size of the conference. International displays are even more expensive. There are big book fairs in Europe; the one in Frankfurt, Germany, is the best known. Inquire about PMA's cooperative display opportunities.

Locally, various associations may sponsor book displays for local authors at local shopping malls.

Time-Geared Publicity

Publicity should be time-geared as well as pointed. By that, I mean that you have to go beyond general releases and plan ahead for greater timeliness. One of my clients was looking to publish and promote the biography of an African-American woman. The book was to be ready in the fall. I recommended that she give it a first-of-the-year publication date because the copyright date would stay current longer. An alternative date for that particular book would have been in

Black American History Month (in February). We chose that timing because the book would be newsworthy on two scores: it would be a new book and it would tie into media interest in Black Americans during that time. (Incidentally, a good source for contacts for promoting and marketing books that deal with Afro-American or Black Americans is The Black Americans Information Directory, published by Gale.)

We knew that local media interest in black accomplishments and personalities would be great during Black American History Month. One television channel aired features every day featuring prominent black citizens. My client provided statements to the media for thirty- and sixty-second segments. Over the course of a month, she was able to gain quite a bit of valuable television time, which was invaluable to her in terms of credibility.

Timing your publicity so it coincides with a specific event can pay big dividends. You can research topical events in Chase's Calendar of Events, a publication listing all sorts of annual events.

Getting Your Books Out

In addition to timely and specialized events, your book might fit into a gift or promotion packet. If it does, you can make use of gift shops, which are numerous, to create promotional opportunities. There are also magazines and websites that cater to the gift market trade, and they often review books suitable for gift stores. For example, my books have been mentioned in *Gift Basket Review*, and one of them, *Letters of Love: Stories from the Heart*, was featured in a gift basket for Valentine's Day.

What do promoters look for when seeking items to include in their gift baskets? For instance, take an organization putting together gift baskets for people who've just had a baby. What better gift to include than a copy of *Nannies, Maids & More: The Complete Guide for Hiring Household Help*? As the publisher of a book for a gift basket, you must give the organization a discount, but obtaining such tie-ins is a great way to sell more books—in outlets beyond the bookstores.

Be as creative as possible in looking for locales for your books. Another example concerns my nannies book. Humana Hospitals of Arizona had what they called the Cradle Club, giving free items and coupons to people expecting a baby. As a publisher, I offered a discount on my books as part that club.

Another promotional opportunity came at a maternity fair, to which the hospitals invited local businesses that provided products or services for expectant mothers. The hospitals wanted to show off their maternity wards, but I also received tremendous publicity from my participation in their maternity fair. The hospitals took out full-page newspaper ads and ran radio and TV ads publicizing the fair and naming the exhibitors. My participation resulted in a dramatic increase in book sales and publicity. You may get publicity and even media interviews at such events.

The bottom line is: keep up with what's going on in your field and your community. Don't be shy about suggesting your participation, because they may be happy to have you join their efforts.

In addition to displaying your book at trade shows and conferences, you can make your participation more economical by offering some services to others. For example, at the International Nanny Association Conference, I distributed flyers from my booth and included flyers from other writers in my books. It brought in extra income to pay for my booth space, and it brought more awareness to other people in the association about what I had to offer. You can benefit by letting people in an organization know you're willing to share your booth and to hand out literature for those who either can't attend or can't afford a booth of their own.

For any conference, brainstorm the theme and determine how you can extend your service to do more than just display your book. Put together cooperative advertising. It doesn't need to be limited to publishers. Consider compatible services trying to reach the same market. If you plan to follow-up by mailing material to your own lists, so much the better.

Be Ever Alert

Be alert for all publicity and marketing opportunities, and encourage your friends, colleagues, and relatives to tell you about any they find. Here's an example. A friend recently sent me a story from the Christian Science Monitor that mentioned a forthcoming Worthy Wage Day. The wages in question were those in the child care field. "Aha!" I thought, "My *Household Careers* book would fit right in."

It was a simple matter to put out a press release with a new head: "Worthy Wages Discovered in *Household Careers*." I revised my original press release slightly to tie in with the Worthy Wage Day and to mention that my book had won an American Association for Career Education citation.

Timeliness was an important issue, since the story about Worthy Wage Day had appeared close to the actual observance date. Therefore, I faxed the information as opposed to putting it in the mail. (That was before email, which would have worked well, too.) Faxing the information was more economical than sending it by Next Day Air would have been.

Waiting for a request before sending a book is another money-saving technique. Editors are inundated with media requests and books, so if you can get them to request a review copy of your book, they're more likely to do something with it than with the thousands of books that are mailed to them every week, month, or year.

For the revised release on *Household Careers*, I selected a dozen of the most likely periodicals from my original list of a hundred or more and then faxed my revised release—and it paid off. Shortly after sending the fax, I received a call from a prestigious publication, one I'd never been able to get a response from before, asking for more information.

To market and promote your book effectively, your mind constantly needs to be working because just placing ads doesn't guarantee increased book sales, and neither does a favorable review. The more energy you put toward spreading the word, the better your chance of succeeding.

Taking something that's newsworthy and is already receiving publicity and tying your book to it gives you an opportunity to gain free publicity, which is always a good thing. Even if only one new publication picks up on it, you're ahead.

Creating Follow-Up

Another way to cash in on an event like Worthy Wage Day is to write a letter to the editor of the publication in which the story appeared. Your letter might say how good it is to see a publication recognized the need for a worthy cause and end with your name and the title of your book. It's another way of getting free publicity, even if the publication didn't actually review your book. It can garner your book both local and national attention—very economically.

Writing Articles

Another good way to market and promote your book is to write an article on your book's topic and place it with an important and widely circulated magazine. There are also many places where you can publish articles online, as well. On the subject of child care, I contacted the American Medical Association and wrote an article for American Medical News on child care. Most individuals, whether they're doctors or not, have a concern for child care. American Medical News accepted two articles, gave me a byline, and acknowledged my books, which generated quite a few sales. The important thing is to analyze a publication and its audience and then gear your article to their interests and needs. Many publications will send you their editorial guidelines, and most of them now provide that information on their website, as well.

Enhancing Your Business

Creating books can be a great marketing tool for businesspeople and can increase awareness and interest about their business. A book can result in requests for help as a consultant. You might not sell many books, but your books can help generate income and solidify your reputation as an expert in your field. Consultations and workshops may reveal a market for complementary materials or even a second book, thus creating another source of income and helping with your book's publicity.

Novelty Approaches

Your book may be newsworthy the first year, especially during the first few months, but what about after that? Winning an award can put your book back in the news. You might sponsor a contest of your own related to the subject of your book. With a cookbook, you could have a cook-off or ask for favorite recipes on a particular theme. If your cookbook has to do with chilies or hot peppers, seek recipes for "The Hottest Recipe in Town." Ask well-known people to be on your panel of judges. If media celebrities serve on the panel, you'll get plenty of coverage of the event, so aim for the media with the largest circulation. You don't have to pay for the prizes, and the whole event could be a fun thing for all. For instance, you ask a local ethnic restaurant to contribute dinners for two as one of the prizes. In return, they'll get publicity for their establishment.

The School Milieu

For authors of children's books or those that might contribute to academic classes or resource centers for a school group, personal appearances at schools may generate sales and publicity. I know of one instance where a children's author set up such a program with an elementary school. He appeared for a day, and sent flyers home to parents, offering special discounts on his books. He even autographed books while he was at the school. Such appearances can be set up as a fundraiser for the school as well as a sales promotion for the author. Moreover, such personal contacts encourage both the reading and appreciation of books. They may also suggest future careers. In that instance, the school library displayed all of the author's books for a week so children and parents could see and review them.

The Instant Expert

Writing a book about your field of expertise can lend both credibility and visibility to your name, but you'll need to have a considerable expertise in your field, as well. Just writing a book doesn't make you an expert on a subject. However, once you've written an authoritative book, you may be surprised at how quickly you become an expert in that field—a status that radio talk shows are quick to pick up on.

Months after your first show appearance, a station may call you again about a related topic within your field of expertise. To encourage stations to keep calling you, it's a good idea to send reminders to stations about your availability and your special expertise. Such contacts will keep your reputation and your book alive in the minds of the media.

Value of Media Mentions

Being mentioned on a popular radio show or in a well-established popular newspaper or magazine column is worth its weight in gold. At one point, I was promoting a Native American book and began getting many inquiries and orders. Although I didn't know why my sales volume had increased so dramatically, I was determined to find out, so I asked one of the callers how she'd heard of my book.

"Paul Harvey mentioned it in his newspaper column," she said.

Checking my database showed that I had looked up Paul Harvey's location and telephone number, had called his office, and had sent information about the book, but that was the last I'd heard about it. After the inquiries began pouring in, I called the program and asked for the date Mr. Harvey had mentioned my book, just so I'd have it in my records for future reference.

When people tell you they heard about your book through a particular publication or radio show, ask for the exact issue or date. That will make it easier for your contact person at that publication or radio program to find the reference, copy it, and send it to you. In the case of Paul Harvey's column, we found that the book had received a very small specific mention at the bottom of the article, but it was immensely effective in generating sales and publicity. A review or an interview is, in essence, an endorsement, and when someone like Paul Harvey endorses your book, it can be invaluable.

Smiling on the Radio

by Len Schritter

The commercial was taking way too long.

I took a deep breath and brushed away a trickle of sweat that was sliding down my left temple. My hand began to ache as I held the telephone receiver to my right ear in a death grip. All the while, the announcer's voice droned on and on as the energetic rhythm of the car dealership's jingle crackled in my ear. The past twenty seconds had seemed more like twenty hours.

Was that thing ever going to end?

It was an early July morning and my first real live attempt at being a book marketer was about to commence.

"Oh, you'll do just fine," my publisher had said a few days earlier when she telephoned me with the news of my first radio interview invitation. "Just be yourself and talk naturally. Oh, and be sure to smile. The listeners will be able to tell if you're smiling by the way you sound."

That sounded simple enough at the time. Smile. I could do that. But when I called in at promptly 6:25 a.m. on the appointed day and was put on hold and told that the host of the radio show would be right with me as soon as the commercial ended, smiling suddenly became the furthest thing from my mind. With the commercial dragging on, my heart pounding away, and sweat dripping off my face like a sieve, it was all I could do to keep from fainting.

Was that blasted commercial ever going to end?

"How did I get into this mess?" I thought.

All I had wanted to do was write a book. That's all. Just sit back and write about what it was like to be a Snowbird in Arizona—the interesting people, the fun times, the crazy incidents. That other stuff someone else could do. Didn't publishing companies have marketing departments? All I had to do when I was finished was sit back and watch people come running to the bookstores, right?

Wrong! I soon learned from everyone I talked to and every article I read on the subject that the number one rule of book marketing was: "Selling is the Author's Responsibility."

"Oh, that's just great!" I remember thinking.

I brushed my forehead with the palm of my hand and wiped the sweat off on my pant leg. My heart pounded away as I took a deep breath. I clenched the receiver even tighter as I realized that the commercial was wrapping up. Then, the cool, calm, friendly voice of the male radio host filled my ear.

"We're visiting today with Len Schritter, the author of a new book, *The Secret Life of a Snowbird*. Len, before we talk about your book, I understand you're a potato farmer from Idaho. Is that right?"

My mind raced.

Say something, you idiot. It's your turn to talk. What do I say? What do I say? I hadn't anticipated that question.

My mouth opened and my lips moved involuntarily as I heard myself croak, "Well, Tom, I don't know what other state I'd be from if I was a potato farmer."

I heard the most wonderful sound on the other end of the line. Laughter! The host was laughing and chuckling at something I had said. I began to calm down.

The sweating and the pounding heart slowly subsided as the host continued, "Well, I'm sure, Len, that there are other states that grow potatoes, but none as well known as Idaho."

More laughter.

I felt myself calming down—and we were off. I sat down and propped my feet up on the desk and began talking. Soon I'd almost forgotten that we were on the radio. Like two old friends chewing the fat, the host would ask a question and I'd answer. Invariably, that glorious laugh would permeate the receiver and I'd relax even more.

Time suddenly flew by. After ten minutes, we broke for another commercial. I found myself once again listening to another jingle, another announcer, but this time there was no sweat, no pounding heart. I couldn't wait to get back on and talk.

Where are you? Come back! Let's do this some more. This is fun.

As the commercial jingle was winding down, the deep, rich voice of the host crackled back through the telephone receiver.

"Today we're talking about snowbirds—what they do, how they feel. Len Schritter, author of a new book, *The Secret Life of a Snowbird*, is filling us all in."

I leaned back in my chair and anxiously awaited the next question.

"So, Len, I have to ask you this. How much input did your wife have on what you wrote? Was there anything in the book that she tried to get you to change?"

There it was. The question I'd been waiting for. For the last several days, I'd been rehearsing how I'd answer that question—in the car, in the shower, when shaving in front of the mirror. I was ready—and I pounced like a cat after a mouse.

"Tom, you're not going to believe this. I had this wonderful chapter written about the snowbird's best friend. It was informative. It was educational. It was uplifting. People were going to read this chapter and go out and be inspired to do great things. It was a chapter about the snowbird's best friend. But my wife wouldn't let me put it in the book."

I stopped talking and a slight chuckle came from the other end of the line. "Yeah?" the host replied. "And what would that be?"

I allowed a long pause before I answered, "That would be Viagra, Tom."

A deep roll of laughter rumbled through the telephone as I sat back, enjoying the moment.

Hey, this wasn't so bad. In fact, it's kind of fun. Maybe, I'll enjoy this marketing stuff after all.

Just then, I caught a glimpse of myself in the reflection of the blank computer screen on the far side of my desk.

I was smiling.

Radio and Television Interviews

Whoever publishes and promotes your book, as the author, you'll be making public appearances and cooperating with the media, and it's comforting to realize that radio interviewers truly need you. After all, without interesting and varied guests, they'd soon be out of a job. Your job is to interest them with a pitch letter, convincing them that you'd be a terrific guest for a future program.

Do some research into the radio talk shows in your area and on the national networks, aiming at those that could benefit from your particular expertise or would appreciate your approach. Few publicity efforts are as inexpensive as doing a radio interview—although few of them will cost more in nervous anticipation.

Often your fear of being interviewed will stem from a feeling of having little control over the situation, but there are ways to prepare yourself for an interview. One of the first things I learned was that the interviewer generally hasn't read my book. That means that in order for me to be a strong guest, a big part of my job is to help the interviewer cover for that fact.

To help interviewers sound as if they're familiar with your work, prepare a fact sheet to give to the person who will be doing the interview. Your fact sheet should include a number of questions that might be asked, in case the interviewer draws a blank, which is never a good thing. Of course, you can't guarantee that the person interviewing you will use your questions, but many will, which gives you more control over the situation because you'll already have an idea of what's coming.

When we create a website for our authors, it includes a media kit. The media kit includes a list of media questions, which comes in handy when one of our authors is asked to fill in for a last-minute cancellation. The interviewer media is able to go to the website and glean all the necessary information to conduct a successful interview.

Here are a few sites Five Star Publications created, offering samples of media kits posted online:

www.ZombieIslandBooks.com

www.50YearsofGunsmoke.com

www.SecretLifeofaSnowbird.com

We have other more generic sites that allow guests to visit our various publishing divisions, as well. Clicking on the photo of any book cover will take visitors to that book's individual website, where they can obtain information about the book and author, as well as a media kit. Those sites include:

www.LittleFiveStar.com

www.FiveStarLegends.com

www.SixPointsPress.com

www.FiveStarSleuths.com

As soon as the interview date has been set, send your fact sheet, press release, and ordering information to the studio. If you're doing a radio interview, make sure the interviewer knows how your book will be available and where, including a mailing address, website, and email address. If you have a toll-free order number, include that, too, as well as whether or not you accept MasterCard, VISA, or other credit cards.

Doing all that makes the interviewer's job easier and gives you more control over the tone and direction of the interview. It also marks you as a pro and increases your chances of being invited back for more free publicity.

Home-Based Interviews

If your interview will be taking place from your home, it's crucial that you have an area set aside that will provide complete privacy and a noiseless environment. Make sure you're not interrupted by the mail carrier, a UPS delivery, or a crying baby in the middle of your interview.

You could put a note on your door that says, "Radio interview taking place from 10:20 to 11:00 a.m. Please maintain total silence. Thank you."

Running your business out of your home may mean that you have both a personal phone and a business phone, and it's important to make sure the other phone doesn't ring during your interview. About five minutes prior to the interview, take the other phone off the hook so it will have time to become silent. A ringing phone in the background can usually be heard during an interview, or even worse, it could make you lose your train of thought.

Have a glass of water nearby if the interview is going to be a long one. Have a pencil and notepad in front of you, especially when you're doing a call-in program. Jot down the name of the person you're talking to. It's more personal to use the interviewer's name as you begin the dialog, and if you're also talking to callers, jot their questions down, along with some of your thoughts. It will help you stay focused and more organized in your responses.

Whether an interview is live or on the phone, make sure you talk directly into the mouthpiece. If an interviewer has to interrupt to remind you to keep the microphone close to your mouth, it can break your train of thought. It also makes you sound less than professional—and in order to be an expert, you must come across as a pro at all times.

Defeating Nervousness

Everyone has a different approach toward dealing with nervousness. I asked Cass Foster, who teaches communication skills, to suggest a few good ways, and in the following essay he offers some great tips for overcoming nervousness when communicating to the public.

As a recognized expert, you may find yourself on a speaker's platform in front of a very visible audience—an event that may be even more frightening than a microphone, a single interviewer, or answering call-in questions. However, media interviews and speaking to a live audience have one main thing in common—communication. If you can communicate effectively from a lectern, you can certainly do it when your audience must be imagined in the lens of the TV camera or tucked away inside a radio microphone.

Cass Foster's suggestions for clarity and enunciation are even more important if you must communicate with very little or no body language.

Public Speaking Made Easy

by Cass Foster

Of 200 U.S. corporate vice presidents recently surveyed, forty percent of those executives said the average business presentation is either "boring" or "unbearable."

This depressing bit of research should serve as a wake-up call for those who find themselves in public speaking situations. It's not enough to be familiar with your subject. You must be able to provide a dynamic, clear, and interesting speech, not merely to sell your product, but to keep your audience awake.

I've taught public speaking for more than ten years. I'm not about to suggest that this particular chapter is all that's required to make you an effective speaker. Obviously, taking a public speaking course would be the ideal situation. However, for those who lack the time or for those who are already fairly comfortable in front of an audience but could use a few pointers, this is for you.

This overview includes controlling nervousness, the ethics of speaking, the use of visual aids, introductions and conclusions, and methods of delivery. There are numerous aspects of public speaking I won't be addressing, such as analyzing your audience, the purpose of the speech, support material, establishing credentials, organizing your speech, types of informative speeches, and persuasive speaking. If you feel deficient in those areas but don't have the time to take a public speaking course, any bookstore will be able to supply you with public speaking texts. A text, of course, won't give you the opportunity to present speeches before critical eyes and ears that are solely concerned with helping you become a more effective speaker, but it will give you plenty of food for thought. You can also contact the speech department of your local college or university and look for a consultant to work with you one-on-one.

Nervousness

When I'm approached to help a student or professional with public speaking, the most common concern is nervousness. Nervousness can be overcome.

Nervousness comes from different types of fear, and it's important to understand that fear can actually be an asset. Fear produces adrenaline, which infuses you with vitality and enthusiasm. Blood rushes to your brain, helping you think with greater clarity. You come across as vibrant and alive.

Fear

Fears that get in your way include fear of failure, fear of rejection, and fear of the unknown. Fear of failure incorporates everything from making a fool of yourself to forgetting everything you had planned to say. Fear of rejection is a tough one because you want to be liked. You want your audience to see you as wise and intelligent. Face it; you want them to like you enough to buy a book. Fear of the unknown has to do with your inability to anticipate everything that might happen, including the outcome of your speech. All these fears are normal, and there are simple tools to eliminate those fears that could get in your way.

Thorough Preparation

Five to eight hours of preparation are required for each hour in front of an audience. Preparation begins as early as possible. This will give you plenty of time to prepare notes and gather ideas. You need to rehearse your speech just as it will be presented, including the use of visual aids. If there's a time limit, be sure to time your rehearsal speeches. (It's common for inexperienced speakers to speed up once they're in front of an audience.)

Communication vs. Performance

Speakers shouldn't think of themselves as actors. Your audience will be there because of what you have to say, not because of how you say it. Instead of focusing on how well you're performing, focus on how you can share your ideas. You want to talk with your audience, not at them. They'll be happy to ignore errors or awkwardness if they're getting something out of your speech.

Avoid Memorization

Winston Churchill began his political career by writing out and memorizing his speeches. One day, while giving a memorized talk to Parliament, his mind went blank. He stopped and started over, but was unable to get back on track. He sat down in shame and never again committed a speech to memory. Speaking from memory can also result in sounding like a mechanical robot. If your audience hears you speaking from memory and not from your heart, they'll question your sincerity.

Check Arrangements in Advance

Inspect the location where you'll be speaking so you can anticipate problems. Do the windows have curtains so the room can be darkened for a slide presentation? Is there a chalkboard? Is there a table large enough to accommodate hundreds of books?

Arrive early on the day of the presentation. Check to see if there's chalk and an eraser on the chalkboard. If you need a dry erase board, make sure it's there, along with pens that work. Test your voice on the public address system. Make sure the lectern is the correct height. Be certain that everything you need is arranged properly.

Concentrate on getting your idea across. "Be here now."

Deal with each moment or point you're making and not with the end result. Some of you may be familiar with Ram Dass' concept of "be here now" from the 1960s. He emphasized the importance of living in the moment, which was a valuable lesson, regardless of what you're attempting to accomplish.

Your body is falling apart to help keep you on track.

Beginning speakers will experience shaky knees, a quivering voice, a flushed face, a pounding heart, trembling hands, a dry throat, and possible difficulty in breathing. Remind yourself that these symptoms are there to remind you how keyed up you are to give a good speech. The audience won't see the shaking, and the other symptoms will begin to fade once you begin to focus your entire attention upon getting your ideas across—since it's not possible to think about two things at the same time. As for the difficult breathing, if you're smiling, your audience will envy you.

Don't apologize for being a first-time speaker or for being nervous.

I was joking about smiling if breathing is difficult, but occasionally speakers experience labored breathing. If it happens to you, you know it and the audience knows it. That's enough. You don't need to tell them what they already know. If you make a point of your nervousness (even if it is by way of apology) that's where their focus will be. You want them to remember key points about you, how your book came about or the subject of your book, not all the ways you manifest nervousness.

Don't expect the audience to laugh or smile.

When people speak to one another face-to-face, they tend to smile, nod, and encourage one another. Not so with audiences. They tend to listen. Don't misinterpret their solemn listening face as not being interested.

Ethics

Ethics, from the point of view of a public speaker, include being familiar with the topic and being honest with facts and figures. Your familiarity with the topic is a given. Once again, that has to do with why you were invited to speak. Being honest with facts and figures has to do with not using data to manipulate your audience.

Visual Aids

Visual aids serve numerous purposes. They can clarify

ideas, make your speech more interesting, and increase your credibility. Visual aids include photographs, drawings, charts, graphs, models, yourself, and computer graphics. The media you work with can consist of handouts, overhead transparencies, videotapes, slides, flip charts, poster, and boards. Particularly for studio interviews, check the facilities for use of visuals.

As an author, I can appreciate wanting a copy of your book resting in clear sight of the audience or camera, but be careful not to appear more interested in selling your book than discussing it. Whatever you choose to work with, don't let your visual aids become a substitute for your speech. An aid is meant to enhance, not to take over.

Handouts can be very useful. If they're short and simple, you might want to distribute them during your speech. Don't talk about the handout while it's being passed out. Longer and complicated handouts should be distributed at the conclusion. They could prove distracting during your presentation. For electronic media, offer the handout, but tell viewers or listeners, slowly and clearly, how and where to obtain it.

When I refer to using yourself as a visual aid, I'm talking about demonstrating things, such as yoga positions, stretching exercises, or tennis strokes. You want to be animated while you speak; just be careful not to allow too much movement to become a distraction.

Make sure you've worked with your aids prior to the speech. Murphy's Law takes over if you don't plan ahead.

Don't think in terms of "How much can I put into my visual aid?"

Think, "How can I make this clear and simple?"

Make sure your aid will be visible to the entire audience or to the camera.

Planning for emergencies is crucial. What happens if the lamp in an overhead burns out? What if they don't have a copy machine to duplicate your handouts?

I recently attended a seminar for the Communications Department of the Maricopa Community College District. The first two-hour period was to be a multimedia presentation incorporating relatively new classroom teaching aids. Unfortunately, all the equipment was stored in a room to which no one had access. The presenter could do nothing more than tell us how excited he was about those new techniques.

A final word of advice. Check your spelling. My first teaching position was with Ohio State University and my first presentation included a poster that read "Warning: This Production Contains Course Material." The secretary to my department chair phoned me and asked me to which course I was referring. The embarrassment and humiliation stayed with me for quite some time. I'm confident you won't allow that to happen to you.

Introductions and Conclusions

The bottom line is to grab your audience right from the start. This can be accomplished with a short and simple story, a joke, a quote, or a provocative statement. I'm purposely avoiding a discussion of the body of the speech, except to say that the body typically contains two or three main points. Be sure to mention those points during your introduction so the audience knows what lies ahead and doesn't have to try to figure them out during your presentation. It's also wise to summarize those points in your conclusion, just before you leave your audience with the point you want them to remember most.

Methods of Delivery

The four principal methods of delivery are manuscript, memorized, impromptu, and extemporaneous. People working with a manuscript tend to read an entire script or periodically glance at a script to stay on track. Giving an impromptu delivery means speaking on the spur of the moment. The ideal and most popular type of delivery is extemporaneous. You sound as if you're speaking spontaneously (on the spur of the moment), but in reality you're well organized and have put a great deal of preparation into your presentation. This is even more important if someone else, such as an interviewer, is in control.

You'll use notes during your presentation, but they'll only contain key words. You don't want your entire speech written out. Making note of important points will allow you to make smooth transitions from one point to the next. Being adequately prepared is crucial. It's easy to get off track and start improvising, but then it becomes difficult to return to the organization you worked so hard to create. Once you begin to come across as disorganized, you begin losing credibility with your audience.

Voice

Projection is an obvious concern for any speaker. You want the audience to hear you. We've already talked about the need to check out the site's amplification system. You may discover there's no such system available. That's where a friend comes in handy. Have your friend sit in the back of the room and act like a third base coach, giving you hand signals for "I can't hear you," "You're going too fast," or "One minute left."

Speech courses deal with things like pitch, rate, pauses, and expressiveness. The bottom line has to do with bringing enthusiasm to your speech, not rushing, finding ways to put variety into your speech, and changing pitch or rate when making new points. The end of this chapter will include exercises to help improve articulation (how clearly you pronounce words) and resonation (the richness of your voice). Practicing with a tape recorder can help a great deal.

Personal Appearance

This is one of those topics I hate to address because it's so easy to be unintentionally offensive. First impressions can only be made once. You're judged by what you wear and that occurs before you present that great attention-getting device on which you've worked so hard. Dress a step up from your audience. Set yourself up as being somewhat apart from the crowd, yet someone with whom they can identify.

Eye Contact

Eye contact creates a rapport between you and your audience. It shows sincerity and enables you to gain feedback. (If they're falling asleep, straining their necks to hear, or looking puzzled, you can deal with it without pausing your presentation.) You'll want to spend about five percent of your time reading notes and the remainder making eye contact.

Questions and Answers

First, you have to find out whether or not there will be time for questions. If so, decide if you want to invite comments as well as questions. Since you need to plan carefully, consider presenting your speech to a few friends and then asking them to ask questions. Don't feel defeated if you're not asked any questions. That usually means you successfully covered everything. When questions are asked, it provides you with a wonderful opportunity to clarify any possible misunderstandings. Questions permit you to walk away knowing that the message you intended to deliver was the message your audience received.

When you solicit questions, don't walk away if no questions are posed within ten seconds. Give your audience time to formulate questions. If the questions are inappropriate or too personal, find a diplomatic way to avoid answering. Be sure to repeat questions before responding. Folks on the other side of the room may not have heard the question. Like everything else, the most important aspect of a question and answer period goes back to credibility. If you don't know the answer to a question, admit your ignorance. Don't fake it.

Conclusion

The most important tool for becoming an effective speaker is practice, practice, practice. The more you speak before an audience, the more your self-confidence will increase. A classroom environment is well suited for practice because it deals with failure more generously than a public forum. A couple of hours, twice a week, at a community college or university could be a wise investment. I've seen the most awkward, self-conscious students you can imagine become highly skilled public speakers in the brief span of one semester.

Enunciation Exercises

I'll end this chapter with exercises that can help put you more at ease. Be sure to apply emotion and feeling with each repetition. Each line should be recited at least three times.

The lips, the teeth, the tip of the tongue.

You know you need unique New York. Unique New York, you know you need.

Red leather, yellow leather...Red leather, yellow leather...Red leather, yellow leather.

I grieve to say your v's are vastly vexing.

The big black bug bit the big black bear.

Tell Tilly, tell Tilly, tell Tilly...Tell Tilly, tell Tilly, tell Tilly...Tell Tilly, tell Tilly, tell Tilly.

It's a pleasure to measure the azure treasure.

How much wood could a woodchuck chuck, if a woodchuck could chuck wood?

Three grey geese in the green grass grazing.

He is bringing the wrong gong from Hong Kong.

Suzie Simpson sits and sips...Suzie Simpson sits and sips...Suzie Simpson sits and sips.

A picket, a packet, a pocket...A picket, a packet, a pocket...A picket, a packet, a pocket.

Resonating Exercises

Sing "My Country Tis of Thee" through your nostrils, plugging one side and alternating.

Place your hand on top of your head and repeat an elongated EEEEEEE sound so you feel vibration on your head.

Place the back of your hand against the middle of your back and repeat an elongated NNNNNNNN sound. Once you feel vibration against your hand, slowly move hand down the back and stop until vibration is felt. The ideal is to feel vibration at your lower back.

If you're unable to sleep the night before a speaking engagement:

Lie on your back and remove your glasses, wallet, and jewelry.

Tighten a specific area of your body, beginning with the ankles.

When ankles are tight, take in a nice, long breath through the nose and visualize the breath as it moves down into your ankles. Once you reach your ankles, hold the breath for the same number of counts spent inhaling. Now exhale through the mouth (as if expelling through a straw) for the same (more, if possible) number of counts and release your tightened ankles.

Use the same process with your calves, knees, thighs, buttocks, stomach, chest, shoulders, neck, elbows, hands, and face.

Don't go through this process just prior to a speech; you'll be too relaxed.

IV.

Marketing
● ●

Co-Opportunities

Co-opportunities is a term I use for techniques I've developed over the years to achieve economical marketing. Advertising is expensive, but often necessary. If you find that you're not getting your book reviewed in key publications, look into co-op advertising. You can arrange some co-op mailings yourself. If you're acquainted with other publishers, you might (as I often do) sponsor a cooperative ad in one or more key publications.

I've had some success with running full-page co-op ads in *Choice* and *Booklist*. A full page can be divided into 1/6-page ads, giving each advertiser a sixth of a page in the magazine. I do the typesetting, layout, design, a picture of each book (another good reason for a design that reduces well) and a thirty-word description. Instead of paying $600 for a 1/6-page ad in *Choice*, for example, you might pay only $300 for the same amount of space because the ad sponsor is able to get a better price and then pass the savings on to each cooperating publisher.

Other sources for cooperative advertising are organizations such as PMA, as well as many state and local associations. These organizations offer workshops or speakers and provide co-opportunities for specific markets. Perhaps your book is geared to educating preschoolers and you want to purchase a mailing list aimed at teachers and others involved in that area. You might search the available mailing lists and discover that it will cost a small fortune to mail 5,000 flyers to that list. However, you could reach them much more economically by sponsoring a co-op ad. Here's how it works:

First, determine your market—the type of buyers you want to reach—and then put together a sample co-op mailing. Then calculate how much it will cost, including buying the list, collating, folding, and inserting the mail pieces in envelopes, as well as the cost of envelopes and postage.

To do it as economically as possible, look into bulk mailing. If you're going to do the mailing yourself, you'll need to obtain a bulk mailing permit and to have your envelopes printed with a bulk mail permit ID number. Contact your post office for bulk mailing regulations and requirements.

If it's a large mailing, you can hire a mailing service to do the mechanical and mailing parts of the job. Once you've calculated all your costs, from printing the envelopes and flyers to all the assembling and mailing costs, divide that amount by the number of other publishers you hope to co-op with. Getting at least three co-op partners will lower your own cost considerably.

You must let each publisher know exactly what the mailing will be and the permissible weight of each flyer. Since postage is determined by the total weight of each envelope, it's wise to print both sides of a flyer. It won't cost any more and you can include twice as much information.

Set guidelines for how the flyers should look. Just one unprofessional flyer reflects on the entire mailing. Stipulate that all flyers must be typeset. They don't have to be fancy or prepared by a graphic designer, but they must be clear, attractive, and professional-looking.

Having said all this about advertising, it's still worth a reminder about the type of advertising to do. Advertising should relate to your product or service.

Revivals

With both publicity and advertising, after a year or two has gone by, it's a good idea to remind newspapers and magazines about your book. Some might not have carried anything about it in the beginning, but even if they did, a co-op ad is a perfect way to bring your book back into the limelight—at a very reasonable cost. You may be surprised at the renewed interest in your book and in the number of new orders that come in.

You may even want to branch away from standard magazines and place ads in those that may have reviewed your book earlier. When talking to librarians, you might ask them to see how many times your book was checked out since it was placed on their shelf. If it's been checked out quite a few times, that library might just order more copies.

An Effective Sales Technique

Here's a sales technique that may result in the sale of an extra copy or two. Charge a reduced shipping and handling fee for additional copies of your book when they're being shipped to the same address. When a customer calls, ask if the book will be a gift. That suggests to customers that they can save money by ordering another copy or two at the same time. You might even consider offering free shipping and handling if a customer orders more than one copy. People love to save money, so be creative. It can pay off in the form of multiple orders.

Seven Soul-Searching Commandments for Self-Publishers

by John Kremer and Marie Kiefer

Now that you know how to publish a book economically, be sure you select the right book to publish. Here are some things to consider before you spend another dime—or another minute—on your book.

1. Be passionate

Are you passionate about the book you're publishing? If you're going to do justice to a book, you need to believe in it. First, you'll be living with that book for at least a year, and maybe five years. Second, if you're not passionate about your book your lack of enthusiasm will be communicated to book buyers, media people, and consumers. It will always show through, no matter how much you pump yourself up. Be passionate. Your enthusiasm will be contagious.

When you think of writing or publishing a book, you'll know it's a good idea if you feel chills running up and down your spine. If you don't feel that kind of excitement about a book, reconsider your commitment to it. You should feel that same excitement with your press release.

While larger publishers can afford to lose money on three out of four books they publish, self-publishers can't. We must continue to market our books until we find the audiences for them. Passion is required to keep us going until that happens.

2. Make it the best

Is your book the best of its kind on the market? You define how your book is the best. Maybe it's the biggest, the least expensive, the most comprehensive, or the most revolutionary. What makes it the best?

The first question that bookstores, wholesalers, sales reps, and book buyers will ask you is: How is your book different from other books on the market? You need to answer that question. If you can say that yours is the best, so much the better!

Remember that the reputation of your company is on the line with every book you publish. Make sure it's the best!

3. Get endorsements

Can you get well-known personalities to review your book? Get at least two endorsements for the book before you write it—or at the very least, before you go to press with the first edition. You can get testimonials and recommendations for a book before publishing. Know the market for the book and then find two opinion leaders to recommend it.

4. Identify five target audiences

Who will buy your book? Identify five target audiences. You should know at least five different groups that would want your book—and you should know how to reach them. What magazines do they read? What organizations do they belong to? What catalogs serve those audiences? What book clubs?

5. Identify three ways to reach each audience

Identify at least three ways to reach each of five or more target audiences for your book, and then decide how you'll reach them. You should work out a specific plan for publicizing, advertising, and distributing to each audience. Which media will you use? How will you use those media? What distribution methods will you use? You need to answer these questions—or at least know how to answer these questions before you commit to publishing any book.

6. Backlist sales potential

Does your book have backlist sales potential? In other words, does it have a lasting market? Don't publish fad books. By the time the fad has peaked, it's too late for most publishers. While there are publishers who made lots of money jumping on a specific fad, I don't know any who built a business based on a passing fad.

Look for books that will sell for years to come. This is especially important for self-publishers who need time to develop markets for their books and to develop recognition for their company.

7. Ten minutes per day

Are you willing to spend at least ten minutes a day for the next three years marketing your book? This is a commitment you must keep.

If you're not willing to spend ten minutes each and every day marketing a book, let someone else do it—someone who believes in your book enough to spend a few minutes every day marketing it.

In just ten minutes, you can make at least three contacts per day. Write to influential buyers. Phone key media people. Network with contacts that can lead to other buyers, media, and associations. Three contacts per day comes out to about 1,000 contacts each year.

If you make 1,000 appropriate contacts, you can't not sell books. I know that's a double negative, so I'll rephrase it. If you make 1,000 contacts per year, you will sell books. In fact, you can't miss.

If you're able to answer each of these questions positively, consider yourself well prepared. What are you waiting for? Take the plunge. You'll never know how much you can do until you try.

The Best Steps Toward Effective Marketing

Have Realistic Expectations

There are more than a quarter million books published in the United States each year—a staggering figure that roughly translates to one book every thirty minutes, every day, throughout the year. R.R. Bowker, the world leader in providing book publishing information, announced that in 2006, the U.S. alone published 291,920 books, and each one of those volumes has to compete with all the others for shelf space in your local bookstore. With odds like that, it's difficult to get any book reviewed, even if you do everything right.

Galley Proofs

When trying to get your book reviewed, timeliness is crucial. Certain trade journals will only review a book in its galley stages before printing. (Galley proofs are generally just photocopies of a book, but it's preferable to have them bound.)

In order to satisfy reviewers who may require galley proofs, send proofs, as well as an information sheet and acknowledgment card, to major trade journals and leading newspapers. Doing this may give you an advantage in getting your book reviewed, and if the reviews are favorable, you can use them as endorsements on your book's back cover.

Book Distributors

Market your book to as many major national wholesalers and distributors as economically feasible. Each of these distributors will have contacts with independent and franchised bookstores, libraries, and specialized book markets, and you want as much exposure as possible for your book.

Discount Schedules

You'll need to develop several different discount schedules, including wholesale, retail, and library discounts.

Media Promotion

At Five Star Publications, our strategy for media promotion includes developing a media campaign and a list of target media markets, divided into three categories.

Media people on the first list receive a full media kit and a review copy of a book, those on the second list get a full media kit and a book cover, and the third list receives only receive a postcard media release.

Postcards

Every new book is newsworthy, and a postcard attracts immediate attention, saves postage and handling, and entices reviewers to request more information. Promote your newest title on the front of the postcard. On the reverse side, include an order form for your newest title, related titles, and a catalog. Interested media people can use the postcard to request review copies.

Media Kit

Make sure to have your media kit prepared before making contact with the media. It should include a one-page press release, a pitch letter, a fact sheet, an author bio sheet, an acknowledgment card, a one-page flyer, a 5 x 7 black-and-white photo of the front cover, a 3 x 5 black-and-white photo of you, and a review/interview question sheet.

Your press release can be fairly generic, announcing the book's publication and why it's especially noteworthy. For example, when we were promoting Passover Cookery, we slanted the press release to coincide with the media's hunger (pun fully intended) for new stories to include in their Passover coverage—and we received an incredible amount of media attention as a result. That coverage was nearly as strong during the next Passover season, which was terrific. However, we needed a new hook to continue that trend the third year, so I talked with the author, Joan Kekst, and asked her to focus on the recipes that were kid friendly. That turned out to be another publicity coup for us, because the media was eager to focus on how to bring children into the kosher kitchen, so they ate it up (so to speak)—and we enjoyed every bit as much media attention as we had when the book first came out.

Your pitch letters can be more region-specific in order to capitalize on how your book fits into a local area. Therefore, your pitch letters generally won't be as generic. However, if you target your pitches carefully, they can be extremely effective and can garner lots of great publicity—and sales. Creativity is an important ingredient in successful marketing, so always be on the lookout for ways you can tie your book into local or regional happenings and interests.

Your fact sheet should include straightforward information about when the book was published, how much it costs, your website information, a brief description of the book, and how a person can order a copy. Always ask reviewers to include your website and ordering information in their reviews.

The media question sheet will help people who want to interview you on television or radio come up with meaningful questions to ask. That way, the people doing the interviews will be able to come across to viewers and listeners as if they've read the book, which is important, because many of them won't have time to actually read it.

Your media mailing lists will need to be customized according to your individual book, so I can't give you a generic list of people and places to send your kit. You can find examples of media kits at our website: www.FiveStarPublications.com. Just visit our various publishing divisions, click on the book covers, and you'll be able to see the kinds of media kits we've created for our own authors.

Using a Book Fulfillment House

Five Star uses a fulfillment house to take care of the majority of our book orders, and your book manufacturer might have a recommendation. Try to locate a fulfillment house that's close to your printer, because it will save you a great deal on shipping—possibly enough to help cover much of your fulfillment charges.

When selecting a fulfillment house, always check their references. You're trusting these folks with your most valuable publishing possession—your book—so treat it as if your success depends upon it, because it will to a large extent. You'd never trust your child with just any care provider, so why would you trust just anyone to help with your literary baby? Start by typing fulfillment house into your web browser and then do your homework. You won't be sorry.

Library Sales

If possible, try to get your book reviewed by a library publication—or at least by one of your local librarians. Scan a couple of copies of *Library Journal* or *School Library Journal* to find out which people are reviewing books for them.

If you can garner a good review in *Publishers Weekly* or *Library Journal*, you may be able to encourage librarians from around the country to add your book to their shelves. At Five Star, we've gotten from 50 to 1,000 orders for books that were reviewed in just one of the major library journals—and those orders weren't just from libraries. We've often seen an increase in sales from Baker & Taylor after a book was reviewed in a library publication, as well.

Mailings to acquisitions librarians can also be beneficial, as long as those librarians have budgets of more than $25,000/year to work with. You can use co-op mailings to help make reaching those potential buyers more affordable; you should include a one-page flyer and an order form in a co-op mailing package.

You can also offer to give talks at your local libraries. Although you generally won't get paid to speak, you might sell books, both to attendees and to the library itself.

Creating a bookmark and contributing to your local library can help get the word out to library patrons—and your kind gesture will also garner attention from other librarians.

Alternative Markets

You'll also want to mail promotional postcards or flyers to industry professionals, to appropriate associations for review in their newsletters or journals, to educational institutions and instructors, to newspapers, TV stations, magazines, targeted book clubs and catalogs, distributors for your target market, bookstores, and to a specifically targeted list of people you personally know who might be interested and willing to help.

The key word, as you may have noticed from the preceding list, is targeted. If your book is about pets, find out what folks with pets read, where they buy their pet supplies and information, who cares for their pets, what websites are devoted to pets, what blogs talk about pets, and on and on. Your task is to explore every avenue available and then to exploit that avenue to your best advantage. You have to reach your audience, wherever they may be found.

In every marketing piece, let it be known that you're available to do talks and seminars about your topic of expertise. Offer to donate a percentage of your book sales to their organization or interest. That will help generate book sales and help get word out.

Book Clubs

Always send promotional materials to book clubs that cater to your target audience. You can find book clubs listed in the *Literary Market Place*.

Book Fairs

The U.S. government maintains an excellent site for locating book fairs around the country. You can access that wealth of information by visiting www.loc.gov/loc/cfbook/bookfair.html. Offer your services as a guest speaker or find out how to obtain booth space. These can also be good places to use co-op techniques.

Catalog Distributors

Sending your promotional information to catalog publishers can often entice them to include your book in their catalogs. After all, they're in business to sell merchandise to a specifically targeted audience, so they're always looking for new and interesting products.

Writing and Guest Speaking

You can generate interest in your book by contributing articles for professional journals or publications. If you're not comfortable writing the articles yourself, you can hire a ghostwriter.

Try to get listed at a speakers bureau and suggest possible speaking engagements to relevant associations. If you're a little shaky about speaking in public, sign up for Toastmasters (if you're a relative novice) or NSA (if you're a more experienced speaker). You can find their websites at www.toastmasters.org or www.nsaspeaker.org.

Conferences and Workshops

You should attend as many topic-related conferences as possible. You might even consider sponsoring a workshop of your own, which could be a good reason to issue a media release. If you sponsor your own workshop, make sure you have plenty of your books available for sale and include ordering information in all your workshop literature.

Book Signings

Book signings can be arranged at various local bookstores by contacting the store manager or the community relations manager for a bookstore chain. Be prepared for a small to medium turnout, especially if this is your first book. Make sure your books are available through one of the bookstore's distributors, because most major chains won't order from an individual publisher. Your book must be available through distributors such as Baker and Taylor or Ingram.

Here's a tip: Contact the store two weeks before the event to make sure your books are in stock, and bring an extra box of books to the event. If all your books happen to fly off the shelves during the signing, the store manager will generally be happy to take a few extra books on consignment.

Supply bookstore managers with posters of your book or a sample cover. Find out what the store is planning to do to promote your event. Provide an 8″ x 10″ photo of yourself, and send a press release to the calendar and features editor of the local newspaper two or three weeks prior to the signing. Try to tie your book signing to a newsworthy event.

Book Awards

Winning awards can be great publicity, so research all awards that are offered in your field. Follow the submission guidelines and submit books in a timely manner, and if you win—let the whole world know about it.

Book Displays

Research trade shows that cater to your target market. Find out the cost to have your book displayed at BookExpo America and American Library Association events. Don't forget local shows that take place in your area. For instance, the folks at Arizona Book Publishers Association (ABPA) offer events throughout the year.

Professional Associations

Send media releases to professional organizations, focusing on you as a member. Each time you achieve an award or mention in a national publication, submit the information to the newsletter editor (of the organizations you joined).

Newsletters

If your company or industry produces a newsletter in your book's field, try to get your book included in an issue, along with ordering information.

Bookmarks

Bookmarks can be great promotional tools. Create a bookmark that's specific to your book with ordering information on the back. Your bookmark can be printed at the same time as your books, using the same stock as your book cover, which can save money. You can see samples of some of the bookmarks we've created for our authors by visiting www.fivestarpublications.com/postcards6.php.

Posters

You can also create a poster for bookstores and libraries based on your book cover. Keep the design simple so the cost will be minimal. For a sample of one of our posters, visit www.50YearsofGunsmoke.com.

Labels and Rubber Stamps

The stamps you'll need include:
- As You Requested
- Review Copy
- Special Fourth Class Book Rate
- Handle With Care—Books
- Return Postage Guaranteed

You may also want to have a label made with your book title. All labels and rubber stamps can be ordered through Five Star Publications. You can get a catalog through our website at www.fivestarpublications.com.

Before You Sign on the Dotted Line

Regardless of who you hire to help with your publicity, here are a few things you should know about the vagaries of the field.

First, believe it or not, gaining publicity for your book doesn't mean that sales will increase proportionally. How can that be? After all, the more people who hear about a book, the more people will buy it, right? Not necessarily, and here's why, from my own experience.

While we at Five Star make every effort to get our books reviewed in a variety of news and information media, we can't guarantee that they'll ever get reviewed. That's because the purpose of news media is to educate and inform the public, not to publicize books. Therefore, we always look for the most newsworthy aspect of our books when promoting them to news media. That way, our books have the best possible chance of getting reviewed.

Another problem is that some reviewers are unable or unwilling to provide book order information in their reviews, which means that customers who learn about your book through a review may not know how to purchase a copy for themselves.

A third reason is that people won't automatically buy your book after reading about it in a newspaper or hearing about it on a talk show. They generally need to hear about your book through a variety of sources—such press releases, postcard announcements, and other sales materials—before they decide to make a purchase.

In Conclusion

Publicity can add invaluable credibility and prestige to both you and your book—at a cost far lower than the cost of a single display ad in a major newspaper. It also serves as a tacit endorsement of your book, which isn't the case with a straight advertisement.

While publicity and promotion can't guarantee that your book will be a moneymaker, without publicity, your book is destined to languish on the shelves. Your decision to use a publicist is the first step toward getting your book noticed—and toward increased sales.

Keeping Track

How do you know if your publicity and promotion efforts are successful? Order response is tangible, but other indicators may be more difficult to monitor.

Clipping Services

For a fee, clipping services will check for particular mentions of your book in a wide array of print media. They'll also send clippings of any mentions of your book or of you as the author. If you're on a very tight budget, their services may be cost prohibitive, but once you're more established, you might find their help worthwhile. Over the years, I've found that clipping services are very good for finding mentions in large publications, but not so good at finding mentions in small or specialized publications. At least in the beginning, your time and effort might be more effectively spent if you encourage publications to let you know when they review your book.

Individual Reports

Another method you can use is to ask purchasers how they heard about your book. You can enclose a reply card with press releases and review copies for editors or reviewers to return, indicating the issue in which the review will appear. Asking publications to include your company name and ordering information will also help let you know where mentions have appeared.

A-Z of Self-Publishing

A is for Advertising. Do very little paid advertising. Try to get publicity first. If you need to advertise, use co-op advertising to share the expense with other publishers, and only advertise in publications that will reach your target market.

A is for Amazon. Once you've published your book, consider establishing an account with Amazon.com. They offer a number of options. Remember when setting the retail price of your book that most distributors will require at least a 55% discount!

A is also for Associations. Join as many publishing associations as possible, since you're going to need all the help you can get in order to succeed. Send review copies and press releases to associations that cater to your market.

A is for Awards. Use *Literary Market Place* to find out about awards your book might qualify for. Awards add prestige, create opportunities for press releases, give a sense of pride and accomplishment, and lend credibility to you as an author. You can also type the keywords book awards into your browser. This may lead to new places to submit your work.

B is for Best. Do it right the first time and then be proud of what you've done.

B is for Book Printing. Get bids from various printers, using consistent specifications. Consider a short run printing (500–1,500 copies) for your first book to minimize your risk and expense. Search the Internet for book printers and make sure to have your book's specs handy so you're always comparing apples to apples. Ask for samples and at least two references, and then check with their local Better Business Bureau.

If you choose the print-on-demand (POD) route, Lightning Source offers a great opportunity to print short runs and then to have access to their distribution channels. You'll find lots of other choices on the World Wide Web, too, but use the same caution you'd use when choosing a local printer.

C is for Catalogs. Get your book in as many catalogs as possible, but don't limit yourself only to book catalogs. If your book would make a great gift, look into gift catalogs, as well.

Check out the *Directory of Mail Order Catalogs*. It's expensive, so you might want to share the cost with another publisher, or you can see if it's available through your local library. Regardless of which route you choose, think beyond just book catalogs. If you're publishing a children's book, look into catalogs that feature products for children, and even if they don't offer books, you could still pitch yours as the first.

C is for Consultant. Establish a relationship with a publishing consultant. It may sound like an expensive step, but compare it to the cost of making mistakes that could have been avoided. Each mistake you make will cost money, and if you eliminate enough mistakes, a publishing consultant will actually save money in the long run.

C is for Copyright. Always copyright your material. Get instructions and forms from the Copyright Office, Library of Congress, Washington, DC 20559, visit their website at www.loc.gov, or call 202-707-3000 during business hours.

D is for Distributors. Do some Internet and Yellow Pages research to get your book into the hands of as many distributors as you can.

D is for Do it Right. Let me reinforce the need for doing everything right. Your first goal should always be to create the best product you can. It needs to be something you can be proud to put your heart and soul into—and doing everything right is the first step toward achieving that goal.

E is for Energy. You need an abundant amount of energy to produce, market, and promote your book, including brainstorming with publishers of similar books.

E is for Equipment. Your office will need a phone, a computer, a fax machine with a designated fax line, a copier, a printer, and other equipment. Economize whenever you can, but make sure each piece of equipment will fit your own situation.

E is for Expectations. Set realistic expectations, knowing that most companies don't make it by selling only one product. On the other hand, every company had to start somewhere. Set a budget—and stay within that budget. Don't put a second mortgage on your home, but if you can afford the risk of investing in your dream—and you're willing to work hard to achieve it—go for it.

F is for Facts. Make sure all your statistics can be backed up. Do your homework or hire an editor to help you verify all your facts.

G is for Galley Proof. The last step before the printer, a galley is a well-written, edited version of your book—not a manuscript that still has to be edited. Send out galleys ninety days prior to the publishing or printing of your book. Make sure you only mail galleys to people who request them. Use galleys to seek endorsements from well-known professionals for your book prior to printing, since it lends credibility to have celebrity endorsements on the back cover.

H is for Help. Keep your local reference librarian's number handy, get familiar with the incredible amount of free help that's available on the Internet, and if you hire a consultant, have your questions ready before you call.

H is for Humor. You're going to need lots of it as you work your way through the self-publishing maze. Maintaining a sense of humor can save your sanity in the long run.

I is for Inventory. Keep an inventory of office supplies, and shop around before you put in an order. Your Internet browser is always at your fingertips. Type in your current needs, followed by the keywords best price.

J is for Junk Mail. You can learn a lot by studying junk mail. Look at other publishers' fliers, see what's effective and what isn't, and learn from their mistakes.

K is for Knowledge. Every step along the way, you need to know what the next step will be if you are to succeed as a self-publisher. The more you know, the better your chances of success, and when you don't know—consult an expert.

L is for List. Be selective about the lists you buy. Proven lists may cost more, but they're worth it.

L is also for Labels. Have a label made with your book's name on it or have the cover made into a label. They're great to use when packaging books. You can obtain a free label and rubber stamp catalog from Five Star Publications.

M is for Marketing Plan. Begin creating your marketing plan from the start. Since your budget will be limited, prioritize your list carefully.

N is for Niche Market. To have the best chance at success, target your book to a specialized market. This book is an example of aiming at niche market. In fact, most of the books Five Star publishes are created for niche markets.

O is for Offer. Offer something extra when someone buys your book by mail. Whether it's free shipping and handling or a 10% discount for buying several books, you'll sell more copies. Find examples of some of the special deals we offer to our customers by visiting www.FiveStarPublications.com and clicking on *Special Offers*.

P is for Patience. Remember that Rome wasn't built in a day. It takes time to do things right, whether it's developing relationships, obtaining reviews and endorsements, getting distribution, or finding buyers. Don't beat yourself up if you don't sell out the first printing two months after publication. When you feel your patience running low, reread R in this list—and make sure you're maintaining Realistic Expectations.

P is for Promotion. Promote your books no more than six days a week, but strive for five days, since you also need to have a life outside of publishing. Don't work night and day—family time is important, too.

Q is for Query. See if other publishers might be interested in publishing your book before you decide to publish it yourself. You'll learn a lot and it may reinforce your determination to self-publish. The Arizona Authors Association has brochures on creating dynamic query letters, as well as lots of other helpful information. Write to Arizona Authors' Association, 6145 W. Echo Lane, Glendale, AZ 85302 or visit www.azauthors.com.

R is for Rubber Stamps. Have several rubber stamps made, including:

Review Copy
Advance Review Copy
Uncorrected Proof
Not for Sale
As You Requested
For Deposit Only
4th Class Book Rate
Galley Proof

Request a free rubber stamp catalog from Five Star Publications.

R is for Realistic Expectations. The first thing to do when beginning the process of becoming a self-publisher is to keep your expectations realistic. If you expect too much you may be disappointed, which can lead to discouragement. Being realistic allows you to lay claim to the many minor victories you're going to experience along the way, and it's always easier to maintain a positive frame of mind when you've had victories, no matter how small.

R is for Reviews. Have your book reviewed by as many sources as possible—including newspapers, magazines, radio and television programs, and association newsletters.

S is for Stamina. You'll need a lot of stamina if you're going to succeed as a self-publisher. It's what has kept me in publishing for more than twenty years.

T is for Timing. Be alert to fast-breaking news in your field and capitalize on it by either getting out a new book quickly or reviving one that's already in print.

U is for Utilization. Don't be afraid to use all the resources available to you, but always temper your decisions with good judgment.

U is for UPC. You can obtain a UPC bar code at: GS1 US (Formerly Uniform Code Council) 7887 Washington Village Drive, Suite 300, Dayton, OH 45459 or by typing UPC Code into your browser and doing some Internet research. The bar code on the front cover of this book is the type used by grocery store scanners. The bar code on the back cover is the type used by bookstore scanners.

V is for Vulnerability. It's a state you may find yourself in often as you work toward success, but being vulnerable doesn't mean being defeated. Keep your eyes on your goal and constantly work toward it—even when you're feeling vulnerable—and you'll succeed.

W is for overWhelming. Self-publishing can be close to overwhelming at times, but whenever you feel yourself being overwhelmed, go back to S in this list and call upon your Stamina to keep moving in the direction of your dream.

X is for eXperience. Whenever possible, call upon the experience of professionals who have been there ahead of you. You don't need to constantly keep reinventing the wheel. Use the experience of others to help you overcome challenges. The price you pay will save time, money, and frustration in the long run.

Y is for You and Your Book. You're embarking on what can be one of the most rewarding experiences of your life—both emotionally and financially—but it's the pride of knowing you've produced an outstanding book that will be your greatest reward.

Z is for Zoo. It may sound strange at first, but once you've gotten into the self-publishing world with both feet on the ground, you'll understand that it often feels like a zoo—welcome to my world!

Publishing most often feels like a ZOO!

Closing Thoughts

Book publishing can be very exciting. It might not fulfill your fantasy of selling millions of copies, but it can give you a strong sense of pride and accomplishment.

My final advice: If you're going to self-publish, do everything with honesty and professionalism.

I hope my book will lead you into the world of publishing with both eyes wide open. It hasn't been meant to discourage you from becoming a self-publisher, but to help you maintain realistic expectations.

If you have any questions or comments, I'd love to hear from you. Let me know the ideas that have worked for you, as well as any advice you may have that can prevent others from making costly wrong turns.

Finally, and most importantly, I'd love to see a copy of your book once it's been published. Here's where to send it:

Linda Foster Radke
Five Star Publications
4696 W. Tyson Street
Chandler, AZ 85226

I wish you the very best, and may your book be more successful than you ever dreamed!

About the Author

"**Every book,** no matter how well written, will languish on the shelf unsold without a comprehensive and creative publishing and marketing plan to support it," says Linda F. Radke, one of the nation's leading consultants in the areas of book production, marketing, publicity, and distribution.

Whether you need guidance on how to begin the writing process or what to do after you've completed your manuscript, Linda will bring more than 20 years of award-winning publishing and book promotion experience to the task. Linda's company, Five Star Publications, offers a variety of ways to publish your book. This includes partnership publishing, a popular option in which Five Star shares the costs and associated risks of bringing your book to the public, and print on demand (POD), which is more economical and allows you more control.

In addition to being the author of *The Economical Guide to Self-Publishing* (a Writer's Digest Book Club selection, Linda also is the author of *Promote Like a Pro: Small Budget, Big Show* (a Doubleday Executive Program Book Club selection). She was recently named *Book Marketer of the Year* by Book Publicists of Southern California.

Appendix

Useful Publications

These are a few of the better known and most useful books in the field of manuscript preparation, publishing, and marketing of books, especially those geared to the needs and interests of self-publishers. Libraries will stock many of these, as well as others, which one can consult at the library or check out. (See Addresses section.)

The American Book Trade Directory
53rd Ed., 2007–08
Information Today
www.infotoday.com

Books in Print
R.R. Bowker
www.booksinprint.com

Chase's Calendar of Events
2007, w/CD Rom
McGraw-Hill
www.mcgraw-hill.com

The Complete Guide to Self-Publishing
Marilyn and Tom Ross, 4th Edition, 2002

Writer's Digest
www.selfpublishingresources.com

The Chicago Manual of Style
15th Edition, 2003
The University of Chicago Press
www.chicagomanualofstyle.org

Directory of Mail Order Catalogs
Edited by Richard Gottleib, 21st Edition, 2006
Grey House
www.greyhouse.com

Gale Directory of Publications and Broadcast Media
Kimberly Hunt-Lowrance, 2007
Thomas Gale
www.gale.com

Encyclopedia of Associations 2007
Thomas Gale
www.gale.com

*Literary Market Place: The Directory of the American Book
Publishing Industry 2007*
Information Today
www.literarymarketplace.com

Time Almanac with Information Please
2006
Pearson Education
www.infoplease.com

*1001 Ways to Market Your Books for Authors and
Publishers*
John Kremer, 6th Edition, 2006
Open Horizons
www.bookmarket.com

*The Self-Publishing Manual: How to Write, Print and Sell
Your Own Book*
Dan Poynter, 16th Revised Edition, 2007
Para Publishing
www.parapublishing.com

*A Simple Guide to Self-Publishing: A Time and Money-Saving
Handbook to Printing, Distributing and Promoting*
Mark Ortman, Revised 3rd Edition, 2003
Wise Owl Books
www.wiseowlbooks.com

Writer's Market: Where and How to Sell What You Write
Robert Lee Brewer, 2006
Writer's Digest Books
www.writersmarket.com

Periodicals

Book Review Magazines

Booklist
American Library Association
50 E. Huron Street
Chicago, Il 60611
Tel (312) 944-6780
www.ala.org

Choice
American Library Association
100 Riverview Center
Middletown, CT 06457
Tel (860) 347-6933
www.ala.org

Kirkus Reviews
770 Broadway

New York, NY 10003
Tel (646) 654-4602
www.kirkusreviews.com

Los Angeles Times
202 W. 1st St.
Los Angeles, CA 90012
Tel (213) 237-5000
Fax (213) 237-7679
www.latimes.com

Library Journal
360 Park Avenue South
New York, NY 10010
Tel (646) 746-6919
Fax (646) 746-6734
www.libraryjournal.com

New York Times Book Review
229 W. 43rd Street
New York, NY 10036
Tel (212) 556-1744
www.nytimes.com/pages/books

New York Review of Books
1755 Broadway, Floor 5
New York, NY 10019
Tel (212) 757-8070
www.nybooks.com

Publishers Weekly
360 Park Avenue South
New York, NY 10010
Tel (646) 746-6758
Fax (646) 746-6631
www.publishersweekly.com

San Francisco Review
185 Berry, Lobby 4, Suite 3800
San Francisco, CA 94107
Tel (415) 536-8100
Fax (415) 541-9096
www.sfweekly.com

Washington Post
P.O. Box 17370
Arlington, VA 22216
Tel (703) 469-2501
www.washingtonpost.com

Small Press Periodicals

Small Press Review
Dustbooks
P. O. Box 100
Paradise, CA 95967
Tel (530) 877-6110
Fax (530) 877-0222
www.dustbooks.com

Association and Distributors Magazines

Forecast
Baker and Taylor, Inc.
1120 US Highway 22
Bridgewater, NJ 08807
Tel (908) 541-7000
www.btol.com

Associations

American Booksellers Association Inc. (ABA)
200 White Plains Road
Suite 600
Tarrytown, NY 10591
Tel (800) 637-0037
Fax (914) 591-2720
www.bookweb.org

American Library Association
50 E. Huron Street
Chicago, IL 60611
Tel (312) 944-6780
www.ala.org

Association of Author's Representatives
www.aar-online.org

Editorial Freelancers Association
71 West 23rd Street., 4th Floor
New York, NY 10010-4181
(212) 929-5400
Fax (212) 929-5439
www.the-efa.org

Publishers Marketing Association (PMA)
627 Aviation Way
Manhattan Beach, CA 90266
Tel (310) 372-2732
Fax (310) 374-3342
www.pma-online.org

Service Corps of Retired Executives Association (SCORE)
1175 Herndon Parkway., Suite 900
Herndon, VA 20170
Tel (703) 487-3612

Fax (703) 487-3066
www.score.org

Distributors and Wholesalers

(Only a partial list. See *Literary Market Place* for many more.)

Baker and Taylor Books
1120 US Highway 22
Bridgewater, NJ 08807
Tel (908) 541-7000
www.btol.com

Ingram Book Company
Box 3006
One Ingram Blvd.
La Vergne, TN 37086
Tel (615) 793-5000
www.ingrambook.com

Quality Books
1003 West Pines Road
Oregon, IL 61061
Tel (800) 323-4241
Fax (815) 732-4499
www.quality-books.com

Mailing List Sources

(Again, only a partial list. There are many others.)

Cahners Direct Mail Service
Cahners Publishing Co.
350 Hudson Street
4th Floor
New York, NY 10014
Tel (212) 519-7700
www.cahners.com

Para-Lists by Poynter
P.O. Box 8206-240
Santa Barbara, CA 93118-8206
Tel (805) 968- 7277
Fax (805) 968-1379
www.parapublishing.com

Twin Peaks Mailing Lists
Twin Peaks Press
P.O. Box 8
Vancouver, WA 98666-0008
Tel (360) 694-2462
www.twinpeakspress.com

Addresses

R.R. Bowker
630 Central Avenue
New Providence, NJ 07974
Tel (888) 269-5372
www.bowker.com

Broadcast Interview Source
2233 Wisconsin Avenue NW
Washington, DC 20007-4104
Tel (202) 333-5000
www.expertclick.com

Communication Creativity
P.O. Box 909
(209 Church Street)
Buena Vista, CO 81211
Tel (719) 395-8659
www.communicationcreativity.com

Five Star Publications
P.O. Box 6698
Chandler, AZ 85246-6698
Tel (480) 940-8182
Fax (480) 940-8787
www.FiveStarPublications.com

Thomson Gale
27500 Drake Rd.
Farmington Hills, MI 48331
Tel (248) 669-4253
www.gale.com

Grey House Publishing, Inc.
185 Millerton Road
P. O. Box 860
Millerton, NY 12546
Tel (800) 562-2139
www.greyhouse.com

Harper Collins Publishers
10 E. 53rd Street
New York, NY 10022
Tel (212) 207-7000
www.harpercollins.com

Houghton Mifflin
215 Park Avenue South
New York, NY 10003
Tel (212) 673-1793
www.hmco.com

Houghton Mifflin
222 Berkeley Street
Boston, MA 02116
Tel (617) 351-5000
www.hmco.com

ISBN U.S. Agency
R.R. Bowker Co.
630 Central Avenue
New Providence, NJ 07974
Tel (888) 269-5372
www.isbn.org

Open Horizons
P.O. Box 2887
Taos, NM 87571
Tel (505) 751-3398
www.bookmarket.com

Para Publishing
Dan Poynter
P.O. Box 8206-240
Santa Barbara, CA 93118-8206
TE. (805) 968-7277
Fax (805) 968-1379
www.parapublishing.com

Prentice-Hall
A Pearson Education Company
One Lake Street
Upper Saddle River, NJ 07458
Tel (201) 236-7000
www.prenticehall.com

G.P. Putnam's Sons
(212) 366-2000
www.us.penguingroup.com

Jeremy P. Tarcher, Inc.
(212) 366-2000
www.us.penguingroup.com

The University of Chicago Press
5801 E. 60th Street
Chicago, IL 60637
Tel (773) 702-7700
Fax (773) 702-9756
www.press.uchicago.edu

U.S. Copyright Office
Library of Congress
101 Independence Avenue SE
Washington, DC 20540
Tel (202) 707-5000
www.copyright.gov

John Wiley & Sons, Inc.
605 Third Avenue
New York, NY 10158-0012
Tel (212) 850-6301
www.wiley.com

Wise Owl Books and Music
P.O. Box 29205
Bellingham, WA 98228
Tel (360) 671-5858
www.wiseowlbooks.com

Woodbine House
6510 Bells Mill Road
Bethesda, MD 20817
Tel (301) 897-3570
www.woodbinehouse.com

Writer's Digest Books
4700 E. Galbraith Road
Cincinnati, OH 45236
Tel (513) 531-2690
www.fwpublications.com